AC (SHELBY) COBRA

Osprey AutoHistory

AC (SHELBY) COBRA
1962-67; Marks I, II, III; 260, 289, 427

F. WILSON McCOMB

First published in 1984 by Osprey Publishing Limited
27A Floral Street, London WC2E 9DP
Member company of the George Philip Group

Reprinted spring 1986

Sole distributors for the USA

Osceola, Wisconsin 54020, USA

© Copyright Osprey Publishing Limited 1984, 1986

This book is copyrighted under the Berne Convention. All rights reserved. Apart from any fair dealing for the purpose of private study, research, criticism or review, as permitted under the Copyright Act, 1956, no part of this publication may be reproduced, stored in a retrieval system, or transmitted in any form or by any means, electronic, electrical, chemical, mechanical, optical, photocopying, recording or otherwise without prior written permission. All enquiries should be addressed to the publisher

British Library Cataloguing in Publication Data

McComb, F. Wilson
   AC Cobra.—(Autohistory)
   1. Cobra automoboile
   I. Title II. Series
   629.2'222   TL215.A/
ISBN 0-85045-554-5

Editor Tim Parker
Picture research by the author

Filmset and printed in England by
BAS Printers Limited, Over Wallop, Hampshire

Contents

Preface *6*

Chapter 1 **Shade tree mechanics** *9*

Chapter 2 **Stranger than fiction** *38*

Chapter 3 **Beauty or beast?** *79*

Chapter 4 **Championship year** *105*

Specifications *129*

Acknowledgements *132*

Index *134*

Preface

So much has been said and written about the AC Cobra that the appearance of another book on the subject almost calls for an apology. The fact that this one is entitled 'AC Cobra', rather than some such variant as 'Shelby-American Cobra', explains its purpose to some extent. I have given the car the name it had originally, researched its history by a study of contemporary records and interviews with most of the people who were intimately concerned in its birth, and attempted to record the result in an unprejudiced way. I have no doubt at all that American readers will accuse me of being 'British' in my approach, and that word is not usually meant as a compliment in the USA. But after 20 years of American writings on the subject, maybe a non-American viewpoint will tell us something new about it.

The AC Cobra has certainly come in for an astonishing amount of attention, considering that it barely reached a four-figure production run and survived on the automotive market for a very short time indeed. It is debatable—not to put things too strongly—whether it was in any proper sense a *good* car, and I encountered some knowledgeable people who said quite forcibly that it was not. One motoring editor remarked that, just as some women had many faults but were fun to be with, the AC Cobra was a very imperfect car that was a lot of fun to drive.

Many sports cars of the not too distant past are now surrounded by a kind of mythology that makes the truth hard to find (and in some quarters unacceptable), but in the Cobra we seem to have one that has attracted a veritable Arabian Nights of fantasy. In one or other of a dozen books we can read how an astute Texan saved a funny little backwoods British company from bankruptcy by hiring them to produce the bare bones of a vehicle that this automotive genius, by dint of a total redesign and using the massive output of an unbreakable Ford V8 engine, then transformed into a superlatively-engineered wonder car unmatched by the most strenuous efforts of the great Enzo Ferrari himself, so that the world's premier sports car racing trophy was borne in triumph to the far side of the Atlantic Ocean.

Some 99 per cent of this saga is sheer poppycock, but its adherents go on believing it and anyone who questions this creed is considered blasphemous. I am quite familiar with this attitude because I married an American and sincerely respect the many fine qualities of that great people, but I learned early on in our relationship that when it comes to national pride, even the French could take lessons in chauvinism from the Americans. Lighthearted comments about American traditions are not well received. Certain articles of dogma must be left unchallenged. I know why it is that Americans believe the first man to fly the Atlantic was Charles Lindbergh, and this belief is unshaken by the fact (as fact it is) that two Englishmen had done so eight years before Lindbergh made his courageous solo crossing.

Such is the power of reiteration that many British people probably believe it too, half a century later. On that basis it can be readily accepted that the Cobra was an American car although it was designed and built in England; that its racing record was outstanding although, even in its best year, cars of half its engine size sometimes outperformed it; that it was tough and reliable although the record shows it needed careful nursing to finish a major race; that it won a supreme world championship title instead of what was actually one of several equal-ranking international awards,

PREFACE

thanks to the efforts of a wily English team manager, in a category where there was no significant opposition from Ferrari.

Even Phil Remington, Shelby's former head race mechanic, said in a letter to me: 'I feel it is about time someone told the truth about the car and some of the people concerned with it thru' its "glory years".'.

That said, however, we must not let the pendulum swing too far the other way when we react to the excess of ballyhoo. It would be just as much a distortion of the truth to belittle the Cobra's impact on the racing scene in the mid 1960s and the reception it enjoyed in many parts of the world, or for that matter to deny that its instigator did a remarkable job in marketing his brainchild. My aim is simply to place on record what I have learned from those who should know, from Phil Remington ('If I were the Hurlocks I'd be up in arms about it, the way everyone forgets AC—but I guess they were just too nice to complain.') to Derek Hurlock, the present head of AC Cars PLC ('You cannot say the AC Cobra eventually became an American design—it was always virtually the same car based on the original AC Ace. But let's face it, it was Shelby who came to us with the idea.').

Perhaps the last word might go to Barrie Bird, a longtime AC enthusiast in Scotland who owns half a dozen examples of the marque and has made an exhaustive study of the Cobra: 'You cannot take away from Shelby his key role as the inspiration of the basic idea, and brilliant exploiter of the Cobra legend. It was tremendously difficult to live up to his sales pitch, but Thames Ditton—bless them!—managed to keep pace and engineer it all properly. I think the origin of the AC Cobra lies around 40 degrees west!'

F. Wilson McComb
March 1984

CHAPTER ONE

Shade tree mechanics

The Americans, whose influence on the English language varies from the abysmal to the magnificent, have a splendid term for the small-time engineer with minimal resources; they call him a 'shade tree mechanic', implying that he operates in the shade of a tree because he lacks so much as a roof over his head, never mind a properly equipped workshop. There were plenty of shade tree mechanics in Britain at one time, though they didn't call themselves that. It was part of our precious tradition of eccentricity that many of them believed they could design a racing car capable of beating the French, Germans or Italians at their own game, and it is a very heart-warming aspect of motor sporting history that one or two of them were right. They could, by heaven, and eventually they did.

The cars they built were called 'specials'. Now that everyone in motor sport works on a six-figure budget at the very least, the 'special' has been forgotten for so long that one magazine recently called it 'a kind of kit car', which was a long way off the beam. John Bolster, who once wrote an entire book about them, correctly defined the special as 'a car built for a specific purpose by an amateur, either entirely to his own design or by combining the essential parts of a number of makes'.

They reached a peak of popularity in the late 1940s and early 1950s when many would-be racers, their mechanical know-how improved by six years of technological warfare, built their own vehicles to combat a continuing UK shortage of cars and, very

CHAPTER ONE

Successful special-builder: John Tojeiro

often, a chronic personal lack of money. Some displayed almost every known error of automotive design, short of having square wheels. Others were brilliantly designed and executed. Allard, Cooper, Elva, HWM, Kieft, Lister and Lotus were among the successful ones that reached the stage of small-scale production for sale on the open market.

Another bore the exotic name of Tojeiro because it was designed by John of that ilk, who had an English mother and a Portuguese father. The car that he built, after an abandoned earlier effort, featured a ladder-

SHADE TREE MECHANICS

Two views of an early Tojeiro chassis showing the tubular ladder frame, transverse leaf springs and wishbones

CHAPTER ONE

The first tubular-frame Tojeiro Special nearing completion. At the wheel is its owner, Chris Threlfall

shaped frame with tubular side-members, 3 in. in diameter, and fabricated 'boxes' front and rear which carried all-round independent suspension by transverse leaf springs and wishbones (or A-arms, in US parlance). This suspension set-up owed more than a little to Cooper, but Charles and John Cooper had themselves taken it from the prewar Fiat 500 *Topolino*. Special-building was like that, with everyone shamelessly borrowing ideas (and sometimes actual components) from everyone else.

The first two tubular-chassis Tojeiros were built for Chris Threlfall, who used a hybrid MG-cum-Wolseley engine, and Brian Lister, whose choice was a V-twin JAP motorcycle engine fitted at the front and driving through a Jowett Jupiter gearbox. Light, practical

and—like most contemporary specials—exceedingly ugly, the first two Tojeiros were so low-slung that some called them 'Catseye' cars, alleging they pulled the studs out of the road surface as they went along. Both won their share of awards in speed events, Lister's sometimes driven by Archie Scott-Brown, a courageous young man who overcame the handicap of severe physical deformity to become one of the best racing drivers we had. Later another car, with Lea-Francis engine, was built for Chris Sears.

At this stage we have to introduce a few more characters into the story. One is Ernie Bailey, who bought 2-litre saloon chassis from Thames Ditton and turned them into handsome big 5-seater tourers known

JOY 500: a single-seater Cooper converted into a Ferrari-like sports car by Lionel Leonard, with MG engine

CHAPTER ONE

as the AC Buckland. He built them in the wilds of Hertfordshire, north of London, and for a time John Tojeiro—who was always short of money—made an extra pound or two by painting them in a barn rented from a nearby *garagiste* called Vin Davison.

Yet another personality on the postwar scene was Lionel Leonard, who reworked a mid-1930s MG Magnette to such good effect that it was almost unbeatable in 1½-litre sprints and races. Having sold the Leonard-MG to a London motor dealer called Cliff Davis who was taking up racing, he then proceeded to turn a rear-engined single-seater racing car into a front-engined 2-seater sports car, which was quite a trick. The

Cliff Davis: the man who drove the Cooper-MG and Tojeiro-Bristol faster than anybody else in the early 1950s

chassis was that of the Cooper-JAP 1100, with the suspension that the Coopers had developed from the Fiat 500 arrangement. The engine was the well-known MG TC 4-cylinder unit. The body was an almost exact copy of the Ferrari 166 *Barchetta*, complete with eggbox front grille. Completed in 1951, the Cooper-MG was registered JOY 500 and took one or two awards before it began to give trouble. Cliff Davis, whose timing was faultless, made an offer for the car one day when Leonard was morosely studying its wrecked engine, and JOY 500 passed into the hands of the man who will always be associated with it.

A likeable individual, Cliff Davis wore a large moustache above a permanently cheerful grin, organ-

Castle Combe, Easter 1953. LOY 500, not yet registered, shares the Cliff Davis enclosure with JOY 500

CHAPTER ONE

LOY 500 as she is today, in retirement at Cliff Davis's home beside the River Thames at Staines

ized some of the wildest parties in London, and drove a motorcar extremely well. The little Cooper-MG seemed to become an extension of that personality, and he remembers it as 'A super car—you could write your name with it on any corner.' Before very long, Cliff had achieved almost complete supremacy in British 1½-litre sports car racing, and began feeling the urge to go faster. He asked John Tojeiro to build him a chassis of the type that Threlfall and Lister had bought, but big enough to take a 2-litre Bristol engine which had previously powered Sid Greene's very successful Frazer Nash. The new car, LOY 500, was finished in time for the 1953 Easter weekend, when it proved extremely fast and won awards at Castle Combe and Goodwood.

As time went on, the Tojeiro-Bristol was not only to beat the Frazer Nashes and win the 2-litre category in almost every race, but was even to give the Jaguar and Aston Martin brigade a rough passage; while a 2-litre Maserati was soundly beaten when Cliff won the sports car race that preceded the 1953 Dutch Grand Prix at Zandvoort. Long before this, he already had such confidence in the car that he thought it should go into

SHADE TREE MECHANICS

'A motorbike and sidecar put together all wrong'—the 1910 AC Sociable

production, suggested to Tojeiro that they should become partners, and made an announcement in *Autosport*. But it didn't work out that way. John Tojeiro, having grown bored with painting AC Buckland tourers, was now happily building another car for his friend Vin Davison, who fitted it with Turner cast-alloy wheels and a Lea-Francis engine.

It seems to have been Ernie Bailey who said, 'You know, John, you really ought to show one of your cars to that stuffy lot at Thames Ditton, and shake them up a

17

CHAPTER ONE

bit.' This was perhaps a little unkind, but AC Cars Ltd were not exactly leaders of automotive design at that time. Their origins went back to 1903, when an engineer called John Weller got some backing from a butcher, the delightfully (if inappropriately) named John Portwine, to market quite an advanced motorcar he had exhibited at the previous year's Motor Show. Too expensive to succeed commercially, it was replaced by a 3-wheeled goods vehicle called the Auto-Carrier which looked a great deal like a 'stop me and buy one' ice cream tricycle. Fast by comparison with the contemporary horse and cart, and capable of covering up to 100 miles on the contents of its 2-gallon petrol tank, the Auto-Carrier sold

Diversity in Thames Ditton products: Cobra Mark III racecar, invalid carriage and AC Sociable

very well indeed, and led in its turn to the first AC passenger vehicle, the Sociable, which an octogenarian friend of mine described as 'a motorbike and sidecar put together all wrong'.

Later came somewhat more conventional cars, and a very successful involvement with motor sport when the great S. F. Edge took control of the company in 1921. An AC was the first $1\frac{1}{2}$-litre car in the world to cover 100 miles in the hour. In 1925 an AC broke the world 24-hour record with an average speed of more than 82 mph. In 1926, an AC driven by the Hon. Victor Bruce was the first British car to win the Monte Carlo Rally.

When the company folded in 1929 it was taken over by the Hurlock brothers, William and Charles, who slowly built the business up again until they were able to market a range of handsome sports cars which did well in British rallies and won the 1933 RAC Rally outright. They claimed that Thames Ditton was 'the Savile Row of Motordom', where high-performance cars could be tailored to their customers' exact requirements, and before World War 2 they had even catalogued a supercharged car as a production model—not a unique distinction, maybe, but something that very few manufacturers attempted.

Even more remarkably, the 2-litre, ohc 6-cylinder engine which powered all these cars was the same light alloy, wet-liner unit that John Weller had designed during WW1 and first built in 1919. It was still in use after WW2 in the well-made but very conventional AC 2-litre saloon and, of course, the Buckland tourers built by Ernie Bailey.

The set-up at Thames Ditton was peculiar. What many people failed to understand about AC was that car manufacture was almost a hobby for the Hurlocks, who controlled an enormously successful engineering business which turned out a bewildering range of products—from aircraft components to rocket launchers to invalid carriages—and made a great deal of money. The design office, of about twenty boards, had

CHAPTER ONE

their fingers in so many pies—some of them positively oozing in gravy—that comparatively little attention was given to car design. Adding to the general confusion, the Hurlocks favoured the disgraceful British practice of keeping executives in the dark about their status and responsibilities. In addition to a technical director, Harold Sidney, there were three designers—a Pole named Marczewski and two Englishmen, Alan Turner and Desmond Stratton—who were never sure which had seniority over the others.

To this disordered but affluent example of British industry came John Tojeiro in LOY 500, borrowed for the occasion from Cliff Davis, the car still in racing trim, and bearing not the remotest resemblance to anything normally seen at Thames Ditton in the 1950s. Marczewski, who had a reputation for liking his own designs best, unwisely expressed his contempt within earshot of John Tojeiro, and when Charles Hurlock mischievously suggested that the Polish designer should go for a ride, Tojeiro made sure he got a ride to remember.

Had the chain of command at AC Cars been different, the whole project would probably have ended then and there. Instead, the Hurlocks offered John Tojeiro a royalty of £5 per car sold if he would allow his design to be used as the basis of a new AC sports 2-seater, which would be fitted with the evergreen Weller 6-cylinder engine. And John Tojeiro agreed.

But, said Thames Ditton, we want a complete car to put on our stand at the 1953 London Motor Show. As there certainly wasn't time to build one, Vin Davison loaned his Tojeiro—registration LER 371—to ACs, who pulled out the Lea-Francis engine and fitted their own, put on wire-spoked wheels instead of cast alloy, brought the whole thing up to show standards of finish and reregistered it as an AC, bearing the number TPL 792. For a model name, AC harked back to the sports car that had won the RAC Rally twenty years before, and called it the Ace.

SHADE TREE MECHANICS

Above *Vin Davison's Tojeiro Special as it was in the summer of 1953, with homemade screen, Turner wheels and Lea-Francis engine*

Left *A few weeks later, Davison's Tojeiro is transformed into the 1953 London Motor Show Ace, with AC engine, wire wheels and all mod cons*

On the AC stand at the 1953 Show, the converted Tojeiro was accompanied by this bodiless chassis, again with AC six-cylinder engine

It was not the first postwar British car with all-independent suspension, as some said, for the 3-litre Lagonda came before it, but it cost little more than one-third the price of the Lagonda and was *the* talking point of the Show. Perhaps the only two people who failed to join in the chorus of enthusiasm for the AC Ace were Cliff Davis, who reckoned he had offered John Tojeiro a much better business proposition, and Charles Cooper, who dug his son John in the ribs when he came to the AC stand and said, 'Look! That's *our* bloody motorcar!' But after all, Fiat's Agnelli brothers might have made much the same comment in Italian, and with equal justification.

SHADE TREE MECHANICS

Vin Davison not only got himself a much tidied-up sports car with a new engine and a new name, but also a new job at the AC works, where he helped Alan Turner with the task of modifying the Tojeiro design for production. Many minor changes were made without altering the basic concept significantly, plus one which was immediately obvious—raising the headlamp position—and one which is amusing in the light of subsequent history—the substitution of AC's cam-and-peg steering for Tojeiro's rack-and-pinion.

The motoring press greeted the Ace with delight, amazed at the way it went round corners and seemed glued to the road, wet or dry, and however bumpy the

Already in production for 24 years by 1953, AC's remarkable 2-litre six was destined to survive a further 10 years

Aces and Acecas in production at Thames Ditton. On the left is Vin Davison, who joined AC Cars when his Tojeiro Special was converted into an Ace

CHAPTER ONE

Two more views of the AC Ace being built at Thames Ditton

surface, compared to most British cars of the early 1950s. *Motor* remarked that it was quicker from rest to 80 mph than any other postwar car they had tested up to 3 litres in capacity. This was surprising, for its time over the standing quarter was 18 secs dead with the aged 6-cylinder engine, then giving 85 bhp at 4500 rpm. Early forays into international rallies and speed events confirmed that the Ace just hadn't enough steam, and the only man who really made it go was a South Coast dealer named Ken Rudd who had his own tuning and conversion business. In his hands the Ace did win a few trophies. But not enough. The obvious answer was to do

Outside the old High Street showroom of AC Cars, a bunch of drum-braked Aces is lined up. There are invalid cars and a 2-litre AC saloon in the showroom behind

CHAPTER ONE

as Cliff Davis had done—fit a 2-litre Bristol engine, which the Bristol Aeroplane Company had developed from the prewar BMW unit to give anything from 100 bhp, in road trim, up to a full-race 150.

Ken Rudd recalls his first encounter with the first Ace-Bristol, in practice for the 1956 Easter Goodwood races: 'They sent it down from Thames Ditton, I climbed in, and the press gathered round to take pictures. So of course I gave them my Famous Racing Driver smile, pulled on my gloves and looked for the starter. I pressed this big black button on the dash and got a squirt of water in the face—it was the screenwasher.' However, he located all the knobs well enough to make fastest lap and win the production sports car race by almost a minute.

During the 1956 season he won over and over again, finishing well ahead on aggregate in the *Autosport* Championship, although the somewhat peculiar marking system gave the trophy to the man who came fifth. The Bristol-powered Ace dominated its class in sports car racing on both sides of the Atlantic, to such an extent that owners of other cars complained it was unbeatable. In the USA it was moved from Class E to Class C, and in the *Autosport* Championship it was eventually placed in the sports-racing category with the D type Jaguars, Coopers, Lotuses and Maseratis. One car was entered for Le Mans in 1957, driven by Ken Rudd and Peter Bolton. They came second in their class to a Ferrari, an excellent tenth overall, and reached 129 mph on the Mulsanne straight. The following year, an Ace-Bristol driven by Hubert Patthey, AC's distributor in Switzerland, and co-driven by Georges Berger, finished ninth overall at Le Mans, and in 1959 the Whiteaway/Turner car won its class, an even better seventh overall.

From early 1957 the production AC-Bristol was optionally available with sorely-needed disc front brakes. The standing quarter-mile was now down to 16 secs and the top speed about 117 mph for the roadster, or something over 120 for the Aceca coupé with the same engine. The coupé had first appeared at the 1954 London

Far left The first-ever Ace-Bristol appears at Goodwood for the 1956 Easter meeting. Driven by Ken Rudd, it made fastest lap and won the production sports car race by almost a minute

CHAPTER ONE

Show and its appearance was much praised, but greater weight made its performance disappointing with the AC engine. However, with the Bristol engine it was a different vehicle. John Bolster of *Autosport* rated it 'For sheer driving pleasure, almost impossible to equal; one of the few really great cars.'

The Patthey/Berger Ace-Bristol was not the only AC running at Le Mans in 1958, for Thames Ditton had entered another which was completely new and bore no resemblance to the Ace. Designed by John Tojeiro once again, it had a spaceframe chassis, a Maurice Gomm body very much in the idiom of mid 1950s sports-racing machinery, and with Bristol engine weighed little more than 1400 lbs. Built in a hurry and completely untested, it met with rear suspension trouble but still finished eighth ahead of its team-mate, being carefully nursed home by Peter Bolton and Dickie Stoop. Later in the year it ran again in the Tourist Trophy race but again had trouble.

Far left *Road and track: the AC Ace-Bristol in roadgoing trim* (above), *and the first Le Mans Ace-Bristol of 1957, which finished 10th overall driven by Rudd and Bolton* (below)

Below *John Tojeiro reappeared on the AC scene in 1958 to design a new lightweight, coil-sprung Ace-Bristol—the first spaceframe AC—for that year's Le Mans race*

CHAPTER ONE

The importance of this first spaceframe AC is that in 1958 Thames Ditton was already contemplating a chassis update. This was a time of rapid development, and in some quarters the earlier Tojeiro design, hailed as modern when it turned into the Ace in 1953, was being criticized as 'vintage' only five years later. Sure enough, at the 1959 London Show AC Cars unveiled the Greyhound, a 2-door, 4-seater coupé considerably longer and wider than the Ace or Aceca. Its chassis was

something of a compromise, the old tubular sidemembers still present but braced by a stout body framework, but the transverse leaf springs had given way to coils, and rack-and-pinion steering replaced the cam-and-peg system normally favoured by Thames Ditton.

The front-end design followed closely that of the 1958 Le Mans Tojeiro, although the Greyhound was designed by Alan Turner. He was also responsible for the new rear

The AC Greyhound of late 1959: a four-seater coupé designed by Alan Turner, with coil-sprung suspension on the original ladder frame, and closely related to the 1958 Le Mans car

CHAPTER ONE

Alan Turner, now in retirement, was the man really responsible for the design of all production versions of the AC Cobra

suspension, which seemed to confuse the motoring press at the time. Really an inclined-pivot trailing-arm arrangement, it was referred to more than once as a swing-axle set-up, and came in for some criticism when the Greyhound was road-tested by *Autocar* and *Motor*, both magazines querying the handling characteristics. According to Turner, this was entirely the result of supplying the car with 16 in. cross-ply tyres instead of the 15 in. radials he specified for the design. However, the Greyhound did not sell particularly well, and whether fairly or not, has been dismissed by most historians as a failure.

AC Cars were also giving thought to alternative power units. Charles Hurlock had encouraged Marczewski to design a range of flat twins, flat fours and flat sixes. These occupied considerable development time without reaching the production stage, and when Turner was called in to solve some of the problems it did not help relations between the two designers. A flat six was fitted into a Greyhound in mid 1961, and parts were ordered for the production of 100 engines, but they were never assembled. Meanwhile an in-line six designed by Alan Turner (and favoured by Charles Hurlock's nephew, Derek) was still further removed from the production stage.

At the same time Ken Rudd began experimenting with the 2553 cc 6-cylinder engine that Dagenham produced for the Ford Zephyr. Appreciably heavier than the Bristol and giving well under 100 bhp in standard form, it seemed to respond to tuning, and Rudd drew up five stages of tune to give the impressive figures of 120, 125, 140, 155 and even 170 bhp. One of these engines in Stage 4 (155 bhp) form was fitted to an AC Ace in March 1961. The car was subsequently tested by *Motor*, who reported that it would out-perform the Bristol-engined Ace in almost every respect. There was the further advantage that while the Bristol was a very 'top-endy' unit demanding a lot of gear-shifting, the rustic simplicity of the Ford engine made it extremely flexible.

SHADE TREE MECHANICS

Above *Derek Hurlock, present boss of AC Cars PLC, backed Shelby's plan from the start but now regrets the Texan's denial of AC's role in designing and developing the Cobra*

Above left *Suitably modified, the faithful Ace chassis (here seen complete with body frame) turned into the Ace 2.6—the real origin of the Cobra*

Thames Ditton decided to go ahead with new versions of the Ace and Aceca using this engine. The ageing twin-tube chassis was modified and strenghthened, road springs stiffened to take the extra weight, and the Ace (but not the Aceca) facelifted in the bodywork by subtly reshaping the scuttle, lowering the bonnet line and redesigning the front. Racing experience had shown that the massive eggbox grille inherited from LOY 500 was too big, so the new car had a smaller and neater forward-slanted intake. As a compliment to Ken Rudd the new chassis serial numbers were prefixed 'RS' for RuddSpeed, the name of his South Coast tuning establishment.

Now almost forgotten, save by knowledgeable enthusiasts, the 2.6-litre Ford-engined AC was a fast and fairly inexpensive sports car of which 45 examples were built: 37 Aces and eight Acecas. Production continued until the end of 1963, and the possibility of using the same engine in the Greyhound was considered, one such prototype being completed early in 1962.

During 1961 AC Cars were of course aware that Bristol were about to switch to a Chrysler engine for their own 407 model. Scarcely enamoured of the still troublesome Marczewski flat six and not particularly

35

CHAPTER ONE

Photographed at Thames Ditton village green (as ACs so often were), this early Ace 2.6 is almost indistinguishable from a Cobra except that it lacks the offset Greyhound wheels and fender flares

impressed by the 2.6-litre Ford ('I never saw a Ford 2.6 perform as I thought a 2.6-litre engine should, though Ken Rudd will probably disagree on that!'), Derek Hurlock talked to Lofty England about the Daimler V8, but he suggested the Jaguar engine, which was really too big and heavy. He also thought of the lightweight Buick V8 and approached General Motors, unaware that Rover had made a similar approach, which ensured that AC's inquiries would get nowhere.

There was, in short, a general air of not uncharacteristic indecision at Thames Ditton, with various executives gazing speculatively in different directions. It was by no means the panic situation suggested by some chroniclers, in which a desperate AC Cars Ltd was rescued from the brink of financial disaster by Carroll Shelby's appearance on the scene with the Ford V8 engine. Cushioned by their government contracts, AC could have bought and sold the entire Shelby organization out of the petty cash. Moreover, Bristol continued to manufacture and supply their D2 engines for some time after turning to the Chrysler engine for their own car. Indeed, AC could still produce Bristol-engined Aces, Acecas and Greyhounds as late as 1963, and 100 unused Bristol engines were sold off by AC when these models were discontinued.

David Sanderson's well-preserved Ace 2.6, chassis number RS5031, confirms that the essential Cobra shape existed before Shelby ever appeared at Thames Ditton

However, the 'Savile Row of Motordom' was not about to turn away business after half a century or so of building cars to special order. In the autumn of 1961, when Bristol's change of policy had become common knowledge, and a letter arrived from Carroll Shelby asking if AC would build him a modified car to take an American V8 engine (which he would supply), the answer was yes. Some weeks later a puzzled storeman knocked at Derek Hurlock's office door to report that he had just opened up a crate containing a mystery engine. 'An engine? What kind of engine?' 'I don't exactly know, Mr Derek, for there wasn't no paperwork, but I think maybe it's Japanese. It says FOMOCO on the side of it.'

CHAPTER TWO

Stranger than fiction

The Cobra's early history has been related so often, and with so many variations by people who had axes to grind or who simply got it wrong, that the chances of arriving at the whole truth now, more than 20 years later, seem slender.

It has been said that Shelby spent quite a lot of time at Thames Ditton outlining his requirements to the men who built the prototype Cobra, and tested the car personally (as he would personally test *every* Cobra, according to his own publicity handouts) before it was delivered. That is not how people at Thames Ditton remember it. Derek Hurlock recalls his arriving—without an appointment—on what he called 'the trolley' (meaning the main-line Southern Electric train service from London!), some time after the first engine had appeared, and well after work on the prototype chassis had begun. Jock Henderson, now retired from AC Cars but noted for his sound memory, says there was barely time to give the prototype a quick run up the road 'to see if it worked' before removing the engine and gearbox again, so that the first Cobra could be sent by air to the States.

It was a tight schedule all round. Henderson says the first letter from Shelby arrived at Thames Ditton on 8 September 1961, and the V8 engine was delivered at the beginning of November. The work of building the prototype began a couple of weeks later, and on 16 February 1962 the completed car was despatched to Santa Fe Springs, California, where it was re-engined

Entrance to the present AC establishment at Thames Ditton is something less than imposing

and tested before its first showing to the press on 10 April. Painted bright yellow, it occupied a prominent place in the Coliseum when the New York Auto Show opened on the 21st.

Another oft-told tale is that this prototype was CSX-0001 and the chassis prefix signified 'Carroll Shelby Experimental'. At Thames Ditton there is a battered brown book recording the chassis numbers of many AC models, issued over many years. It reveals that AC Cars Ltd, like most car manufacturers, never began a new series with number one, and the prototype was in fact CSX-2000. The letters CS certainly meant Carroll Shelby (though the junior employee who kept the records rendered it as 'Carol Shelby', some way short of the usual macho image). As for the X, this had for years been AC's way of denoting an export order, usually with left-hand drive.

Shelby's denial of the 'export' tag, signifying 'import' on the other side of the Atlantic, must have been inevitable by late 1965 when the Cobra was getting the full publicity treatment as an all-American, championship winning car. The commercial or competition success of imported cars had long been a sore subject

CHAPTER TWO

Right and below *The prototype Cobra under construction at Thames Ditton*

40

with the more rednecked of the America-first brigade, and Shelby was certainly not the first to compromise by stuffing a big-displacement American engine into a British sports car. Sydney Allard and Donald Healey had begun exporting engineless cars to the USA a good 10 to 15 years earlier—and with Mercury, Nash or Cadillac horsepower, they accomplished more in out-and-out sports car racing than any Shelby car was later able to do. In those days, American race reporters invented the word 'British-bodied' for such vehicles—as if steering, brakes and suspension had nothing to do with their success.

It was part of the same process to depreciate AC's role in designing the car by saying that Shelby, backed by Ford's technical expertise, had to rethink the chassis from end to end. 'The entire car was redesigned around the engine,' writes one of his disciples. This simply isn't true. What Ford knew about sports car design in the early 1960s was clearly revealed to the world when the appalling Mustang made its appearance in April 1964. And most of the changes in the original Ace specification had been made *before the Cobra came into existence*, being related to the design of the Greyhound and the Dagenham Ford-engined Ace and Aceca 2.6. Of the entire production of 2.6-litre cars, only one (and that an Aceca) was exported new to the USA. The Greyhound, too, was virtually unknown, so there is some excuse for American unfamiliarity with these models, which might be described as the missing link between Ace and Cobra.

As mentioned earlier, the reshaping of the body and the new frontal treatment that so many associate with the Cobra had already appeared on the Ace 2.6—which, however, lacked the Cobra's fender flares. We are told that the transverse springs and wishbones were lengthened to increase the track (tread). They were not; the difference is accounted for by the use of Greyhound wheels, which had a wider offset. The Cobra did have thicker kingpins or swivel-pins than the original Ace, but these had been introduced for the 2.6; it didn't help

CHAPTER TWO

A close-up of the prototype Cobra shows the inboard disc brakes at the rear end

that in Thames Ditton terminology they were 'spindles', which made most people think of stub-axles or hub spindles. The main chassis tubes were 12 SWG thick on the Cobra instead of 14, but this change had come with the original Aceca. The front brake discs, described as being of 12 in. diameter in Shelby literature, were in fact 11.63 in., as they had been since the days of the Ace-Bristol, and the same Girling Type B calipers were fitted.

In short, the front end of the original Cobra chassis was pure AC Ace 2.6 apart from the mounting of the (identical) steering box, which had to be canted to one side to clear the wider V8 engine. The back end obviously had to be redesigned to take the Salisbury 4HU differential instead of the old ENV unit, and for some reason Shelby specified inboard disc brakes. This was no problem at all: the mountings were already there, as inboard discs were also used on the Jaguar Mark 10 and E type, for which the unit had been designed. Nevertheless ACs had misgivings, knowing the problems of overheating and poor accessibility that they

42

presented, and all subsequent Cobras had outboard discs at the rear. Actually 10.75 in. in diameter, they too grew to 12 in. in the Shelby brochures, although even the race cars and the 427-engined Cobras never had discs that big, front or back.

There is a small mystery in connection with the building of the prototype. All the drawings produced by AC's drawing-office are marked 'Ace 3.6', and we know that Shelby originally meant the car to be powered by the Fairlane 221 cu. in. engine, which is 3622 cc capacity in metric measure as used in Britain—approximately 3.6 litres. However, it was just about the time of Shelby's first approach to AC that Ford decided to phase out the 221-cube engine in favour of the 260 (4261 cc, loosely but incorrectly known as 4.2 litres) and 289 (4736 cc, approximately 4.7 litres). The engine sent over for the prototype lay around the AC works for years, and was eventually bought by ACOC member Barrie Bird to use in an early Cobra he was rebuilding. By measuring the bores he confirmed that it was a 260, but there is nothing

An AC works note suggests this is Cobra Number 9, one of two cars flown to Los Angeles on 8 August 1962

CHAPTER TWO

AC Form 54

elephone : EMBERBROOK 5621
Telegrams: AUTOCARRIER, THAMES DITTON.

Please quote this number on any relative communication.
A 7176

Shelby American Inc.,
1042 Princeton,
Venice, California, U.S.A.

Date 22nd October, 1962.
Ref. RGH/HP

IN ACCOUNT WITH

AC CARS LIMITED
HIGH STREET, THAMES DITTON, SURREY

Chassis/Car No.	Engine No.	Registered No.	£	s.	d.	£	s.	d.
CSX2033								

To supplying:-

One A.C. Ace Cobra cellulosed in White with Red trim, top and tonneau, completed to specification dated 17th July, 1962.   890 - -

To supplying and fitting:-

Prop Shaft   3   -   -
4 tyres and tubes 19 9   -
Heater   14 2   6
                   926 11 6
Less speedo drive not fitted 1 15 -
                   924 16 6
Special packing for windscreen 2 10 -
Delivery to Docks 5   -   -
                                        £932 6 6
Less deposit already received   78 4 6
                                        £854 2 -

TERMS OF PAYMENT

Settlement is due on receipt of advice that car is ready for delivery (Rendition of invoice nally coincides with this advice).

...tomers are respectfully advised that Cheques tendered in payment must be in the Company's possession at least FIVE clear working days before delivery of Car is taken.

Any objection to, or complaint regarding the charges in this invoice must be made within SEVEN DAYS of the date hereon, otherwise it cannot be entertained.

external to distinguish the engine from a 221 if one is unfamiliar with these V8s. It seems quite likely that ACs (who had no occasion to remove the heads) believed all along that they were dealing with a 221. Hence, perhaps, the 'Ace 3.6' tag on the drawings and a trace of uncertainty about the engine capacity that still lingers on today.

Further confusion is caused by loosely referring to different Cobra models as 260, 289, 427 and so on in the USA, and 4.2-litre, 4.7-litre or 7-litre in the UK, with the added complication that 'Mark II' means a coil-sprung Cobra in AC's own chassis record book but a leaf-sprung car to the company's drawing-office or stores. The only satisfactory system is to define the models by their

Far left *AC Cars Ltd invoice to Shelby American Inc for Number 33 totals £932 6s 6d, including just over £44 for tyres, tubes, heater and delivery to the docks*

Above *The boys in their shiny suits: a very youthful Phil Hill, Dan Gurney and Carroll Shelby with an early Cobra in California*

CHAPTER TWO

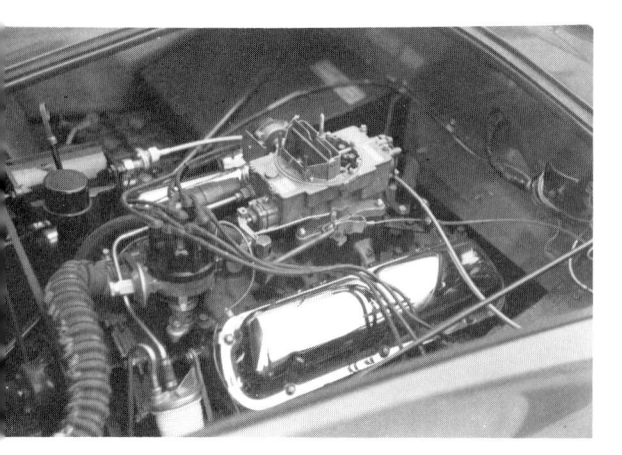

A stock 289 engine in a Mark I (above) and an experimental 427 in a racing Mark III (above right)

chassis instead of their engines—especially as so many 260-engined cars have been converted to 289s or the later 302s, many so-called 427s are in reality 428s, and what Europeans call an AC289 is essentially a 427 to Americans.

On this basis the Mark I Cobra is the original version with transverse leaf springs and Bishop cam-and-peg steering (also known as worm-and-sector). The first 75 of these (including the prototype) were fitted with 260-cube engines on arrival in the USA, although one, CS-2030, was retained by Thames Ditton as a demo car, and according to one source had rack-and-pinion steering from the start. The remaining 51 Mark I models were all fitted with 289-cube engines, which must have become generally available to Shelby in the early part of 1963.

Towards the end of 1962, Alan Turner managed to complete a fairly major design exercise at the front end to provide the Cobra with rack-and-pinion steering while retaining the transverse leaf spring, and this chassis went into production early in 1963 as the Cobra Mark II. To achieve this change with reasonable suspension geometry, the front wishbones were made shorter and their pivot points more widely spaced, while the uprights and spring connections were altered considerably. All Mark II Cobras were originally fitted

STRANGER THAN FICTION

Works pictures of the Mark I (left) and Mark II (below) chassis, photographed for use in the manuals

CHAPTER TWO

Mark I cam-and-peg steering is revealed by the flat Mark I steering wheel with equidistant spokes (right); Mark II rack-and-pinion steering by the dished Mark II wheel with asymmetric spoke pattern (below)

Transverse-leaf rear suspension of the Cobra Mark I and Mark II

with 289 engines in the USA, but in view of the many engine changes made subsequently it is convenient to remember one simple recognition feature—the steering wheel. The Mark II wheel had three spokes asymmetrically placed at 9, 6 and 3 o'clock so that two of them made a straight line. The Mark I also had three spokes, but they were evenly spaced at 12, 4 and 8 o'clock. Moreover, the Mark II wheel was dished, the Mark I flat, and one cannot be changed for the other.

Total Mark II production looks like 528 cars, but the records are not clear enough to allow dogmatism on this point. There is considerable confusion in AC's own records, and the situation has since become hopelessly clouded as new Cobras are continually 'discovered' in response to their steadily rising market value; some numbers have been duplicated or acquired a suffix letter, and one Cobra is reputed to carry the chassis number of an AC invalid carriage! The last genuine leaf-sprung cars were built in November 1964 for the USA, but continued into the summer of 1965 for the European market.

The designation 'Mark III' seems logical for the coil-spring Cobra, the first examples of which were shipped to

CHAPTER TWO

the USA in October 1964. Although this model was known as the 427 in America, many were actually fitted with the cheaper and much less powerful 428 engine; it seems that no records survive to reveal how many, exactly, and some Cobra enthusiasts have put forward a simple (but unrepeatable) explanation for their absence. Completion of coil-sprung cars ground to a halt in California as Shelby turned his attention to other more promising money-spinners, but in Europe there was still a modest demand for the car. The name of Cobra having been bought by Ford for use on a later version of the Mustang, Thames Ditton decided to call it the AC289—the 289 engine being considered quite big enough for European requirements—and succeeded in selling 27 more cars before doing a major revamp by adding 6 in. to the wheelbase, fitting a Frua-designed body and a 428 engine, and selling this as the AC428 with a CF (Cobra Frua) chassis prefix. Excluding the AC428 and a number of oddball derivatives built to special order, the total of coil-sprung Cobras would appear to be 344 cars. AC Cars admit they were exaggerating when they talked airily of 1500 to 2000 Cobras being built, and it is difficult to see how others arrive at 1140 or even 1011; the genuine total would seem to be something under 1000 cars.

The Mark III Cobra is a car that has come in for some pretty extravagant praise: 'The absolute all-time king of street cars. . . . Whatever the 289 did well, the 427 did better.' 'Far superior to the leaf-spring models in every respect except possibly gas mileage. Any faults that the earlier Cobras had were corrected, and all of the things that made a Cobra were retained.' Some American enthusiasts, in their admiration for the Mark III, have even suggested that the earlier models were not all that different from an Ace-Bristol—which in the USA is a well-nigh subversive thing to say.

The first big-engined Cobra was a Mark II fitted with a 427 engine, and run, as an experiment, in the Sebring 12 Hours of 1964. The drivers, Ken Miles and John Morton, swore it handled like a 1948 Buick, and Miles proved the

STRANGER THAN FICTION

Left *Coil springs and wishbones at the rear of the Cobra Mark III*

Below *Front view of the beefy Mark III chassis with its wider-spaced and larger-diameter chassis tubes*

CHAPTER TWO

An early Mark II photographed—as always—on Thames Ditton village green

STRANGER THAN FICTION

CHAPTER TWO

The first rhd Cobra, CS-2030 was a works demo car built during the Mark I period but seemingly with Mark II steering

point during practice by hitting a tree—not an easy thing to do in the featureless desert that is Sebring. Everyone was delighted when the engine threw a rod and they felt free to retire from the race before hitting anything else, for statistically the anything else was liable to be another competitor.

The production Mark III began its life on 1 January 1965, after the two prototypes had been sent to the States in October 1964. The main chassis tubes, enlarged from 3 to 4 in. in diameter, were also spaced $2\frac{1}{2}$ in. further apart. The suspension towers were fabricated in tube instead of steel plate, and carried wishbones top and bottom. The coil springs which had replaced the transverse leaves were concentric with the shock absorbers. Hubs, bearings and half-shafts were all stronger than before, but the differential unit was the same. As the first Mark III models were intended to be race cars, they also had the bigger racing brakes.

In appearance the Mark III was altogether more aggressive, though the facelift was cleverly done in such a way that the cost of the change was minimized: windscreen, doors, bonnet (hood) and trunk-lid were all

Mark II components. However the body was wider, and seemed wider still with pronounced flares in the wings (fenders) to accommodate the wide-rim Halibrand wheels fitted to most of the cars. The frontal intake was bigger and, again, seemed bigger still because it was open, the eggbox grille having given way to a simple horizontal plate called an air-splitter, which was supposed to improve flow though the radiator. It was flanked by vertical intakes, and usually there was a box-like arrangement underneath to take an oil-cooler—a multiplicity of air-intakes being fashionable at this time, although one or other was masked by the fitting of a number-plate. The Mark III was substantially heavier than the original Cobra. Road test figures indicate six or seven times the 50 lb difference quoted in Shelby specifications.

Wider fender flates and a new front made the Mark III seem much more aggressive—but this, strictly, is a 'Mark IV', one of the Autokraft replicars (note the AC badge)

CHAPTER TWO

We are told that the coil-sprung Cobra was entirely a Ford design, computer-defined with such exactitude that the result was perfection. In the words of one American editor, 'Nothing—not one thing—had to be changed.' If he had ever visited Thames Ditton he would have heard a slightly different story. Derek Hurlock said: 'Well, I don't want to upset anybody, but my feeling is that Alan Turner did a lot more than is generally realized. True, Ford sent Bob Negstadt over, and Shelby had Phil Remington with us at the time—Phil was a marvellous bloke who gave us real, practical help in the development of that car. He wasn't involved in the calculations on suspension—that came from Ford's computer. But Alan Turner had to rehash a lot of that, because it just wouldn't work in practice.' Phil Remington himself, still working for All-American Racers Inc at the old plant in Venice, California, told me: 'Bob Negstadt did much of the suspension, along with Alan Turner, but I don't think they used much of the computer work. Ford's computer was about the size of two automotive garages at that time, but I don't think it was really working well enough to do the job.'

Alan Turner, when I first approached him, remembered that the Ford computer was initially involved in the rear suspension design: 'It supplied us with some ideal locations for the wishbone pivot centres, inner and outer, but when I came to lay this out, to design a suspension around this information, I found the forward pivot points were located about the middle of the driver's and passenger's bodies! I had to design it all over again, and it took 10 to 14 days to work it out—*without* a computer.'

It has also been suggested that the rear suspension of the Mark III Cobra originated with a design that Klaus Arning (then with Ford Germany) produced for the first Mustang prototype—a mid-engined car that could scarcely be more different from the production Mustang, although an independent rear suspension was promised for racing versions of the Shelby Mustang, but never

Above *Phil Remington: 'A marvellous bloke, and a real gentleman,' said AC chief Derek Hurlock*

Far left *Road and track again: the Cobra Mark III in roadgoing* (above) *and racegoing* (below) *form. Strangely, the racecar has a Mark II rollover bar with strut angled forward instead of back*

actually materialized. Alan Turner's reaction to this is interesting: 'Having read the article which you sent to me, I have no doubt that the suspension system developed by Klaus Arning must have been the basis used to produce the computer read-out defining the desired positions for the linkage pivot points of the 427 Cobra suspension. Geometrically, the system shown . . . is the same as that on the Cobra. So, too, is the Mustang irs shown, but in design it is very different from the Cobra. . . . It is a case of confusing invention with design. The suspension of the Cobra 427 was designed by me to largely conform to a computer-determined geometry (by Ford) of a system invented by Klaus Arning: that would appear to be a fair way of putting it!'

Klaus Arning's comment on Alan Turner's letter was: 'He is correct in stating that the final rear suspension hardware design for the 427 Cobra was executed by AC Cars Ltd around the geometry provided by us. However, we made preliminary design studies here [at Dearborn] of the new chassis, front and rear suspension. But these had to be very much revised, mainly because of the AC's understandable intent to incorporate as many "off the shelf" hardware items in the "production" version as practicable. They succeeded in this without significant changes in the resulting suspension geometry characteristics.'

In conversation with me, Turner also remarked: 'It's one thing to produce an ideal system of location points where all the wishbones and draglinks should pivot, but it's another thing to put it into practice—and that, really, is what we at ACs did. All we had was a computer print-out and one or two graphs showing wheel movements; we had to do everything else before we could turn out the production drawings. But of course when you're selling cars to the Americans, as Shelby was, the more "American" you can make them seem, the more appeal they would have.'

During the early life of the Cobra things were different, for then Shelby did not hesitate to make use of

AC's reputation. The very first press release refers to the car as the 'Shelby AC Cobra' and calls it 'A unique and effective combination of a modern American production powerplant and a renowned English sports car body and chassis.' It said 'Planning the Cobra, Shelby consulted with the AC Car Company of England and designed his new sports car around what he believes is the best-handling production car chassis in the world, powered by a modern American engine that has the stamina to meet the requirements of road racing. . . . The chassis, running gear, body, upholstery, appointments and trim to the finish color coat of paint are completed by the AC Car Company in Thames Ditton, Surrey, England. The Ford engines will be installed when the cars reach Los Angeles, and Shelby will test-drive each Cobra before delivery.' The same press release asserted that 'Coachwork and trim are of the same high quality which characterized the AC-Bristol and Aceca cars . . . . Although this chassis has been redesigned to accept the greater power output of the 260 cu. in. Ford V-8, the car has the same large-tube frame and independent suspension that gave *other* AC cars a notable reputation for handling.' My italics for that interesting word 'other'.

Even when Shelby (despite his agreement with AC Cars Ltd to use their name) removed the stock AC badges from the cars and substituted his own, the first design of badge that he fitted did, at least, incorporate the letters AC along with the words 'Shelby Cobra'. Remarkably forbearing, AC agreed to discontinue fitting their own badge (which, being bigger, left visible holes that were difficult to hide), but the Shelby AC Cobra badge was replaced in its turn by one bearing only the word Cobra. Asked his opinion of this substitution, Derek Hurlock said: 'It's true, he should have left our badge on. We were very fed up about it at the time, but it was typical of Carroll Shelby—he was like that; it was one of his failings. So we said well, it's the nature of the guy, and being British we let him get away with it.'

CHAPTER TWO

BUY IT!.....OR WATCH IT GO BY!

SHELBY AC COBRA POWERED BY FORD

STRANGER THAN FICTION

For the record, let it be stated quite simply that each Cobra—whether Mark I, II or III—began life in a distinctly archaic-looking section of the AC works where cold-drawn mild steel tube was cut to length and bent in *wooden* presses which were hand-operated. Radiused at the ends as required, the tubes were then fitted in an assembly jig and arc-welded, but the body framework (a mixture of round and square tubing) was gas-welded to the main frame. Steering shafts, suspension members and wheel hubs were made in AC's own machine-shop, which in those days was capable of producing almost anything.

Body panels were wheeled (not beaten) to shape, in small sections, by several outside contractors. They were then welded together into larger panels on a mock-up, fitted to the body-frame and riveted to it when the fit

Far left and above *Original Shelby catalogue stressed the part played by 'the famed AC Car company', pictured the prototype car with different over-riders front and rear. The chassis shown is actually that of the Ace 2.6, not the Cobra!*

61

CHAPTER TWO

was correct, after which all the welds had to be wire-brushed. Painting was a lengthy process that began with an etch primer on the aluminium body, followed by five thick coats of filler, a neutralizing sealer, then about five coats of colour, rubbed down by hand between coats (Shelby's press release made it 12 coats of acrylic lacquer in all). Seat frames were hand-upholstered, using Bridge of Weir hides, and there was virtually no flow-production of trim panels or carpeting; even the hood-sticks were hand-fitted to suit each individual car, while the eggbox front grilles and wood-and-ali steering

STRANGER THAN FICTION

Cobras in production at Thames Ditton, on the same assembly line seen on page 26

wheels were also made up at Thames Ditton.

Not surprisingly, the assembly time that went into each car totalled four weeks or more, but Shelby himself said 'Anything built in England is about a third of the cost here. We build what we can overseas because of savings in using European labor.' What Thames Ditton turned out, then, was a complete car minus engine and gearbox, and the regular output of Cobras was 12 cars per week. Normally they were delivered to the docks on two double-decker trailers, each with three cars above and three below, and shipped to California. Sometimes

CHAPTER TWO

Far right *AC tradition: the post-WW2 two-door 2-litre saloon, designed and built at Thames Ditton*

Below *Panelling body frames in another part of the AC works*

they went straight to Ed Hugus, Shelby's East Coast distributor, or to Italy as a chassis for special bodywork, or to Detroit for FoMoCo to play around with them. Sometimes they were air-freighted if time was short. Usually a protective wooden board was fitted front and back, bolted to the over-rider brackets and with the destination painted on it. The windscreen was stowed inside the cockpit for its protection, and whether the car had splined hubs to take centrelock wire wheels or peg-drive hubs for Halibrands, it was usually sent out on slave wheels. Returned from the USA in intermittent

The Saloon

LOUNGE comfort and ample accommodation for five people is the keynote of this modern styled body. The upholstery, trimmings and fittings are of the finest quality.

The controls come to hand with an easy facility, the steering and seating are adjustable.

Ease of entry and exit for the rear passengers is not hindered by the front seats; an unusual feature in a two-door Saloon. Visibility in all directions is exceptional, adding greatly to the driving safety and passengers' enjoyment. A wide platform by the rear windows takes gloves, hats, bags, etc.

An altogether exceptional body designed and built in the A.C. Works.

Except for some extra air intakes because it has a racecar body, the genuine Cobra Mk III of 1965 (right) and the Autokraft Mk IV (above) of 20 years later look very alike

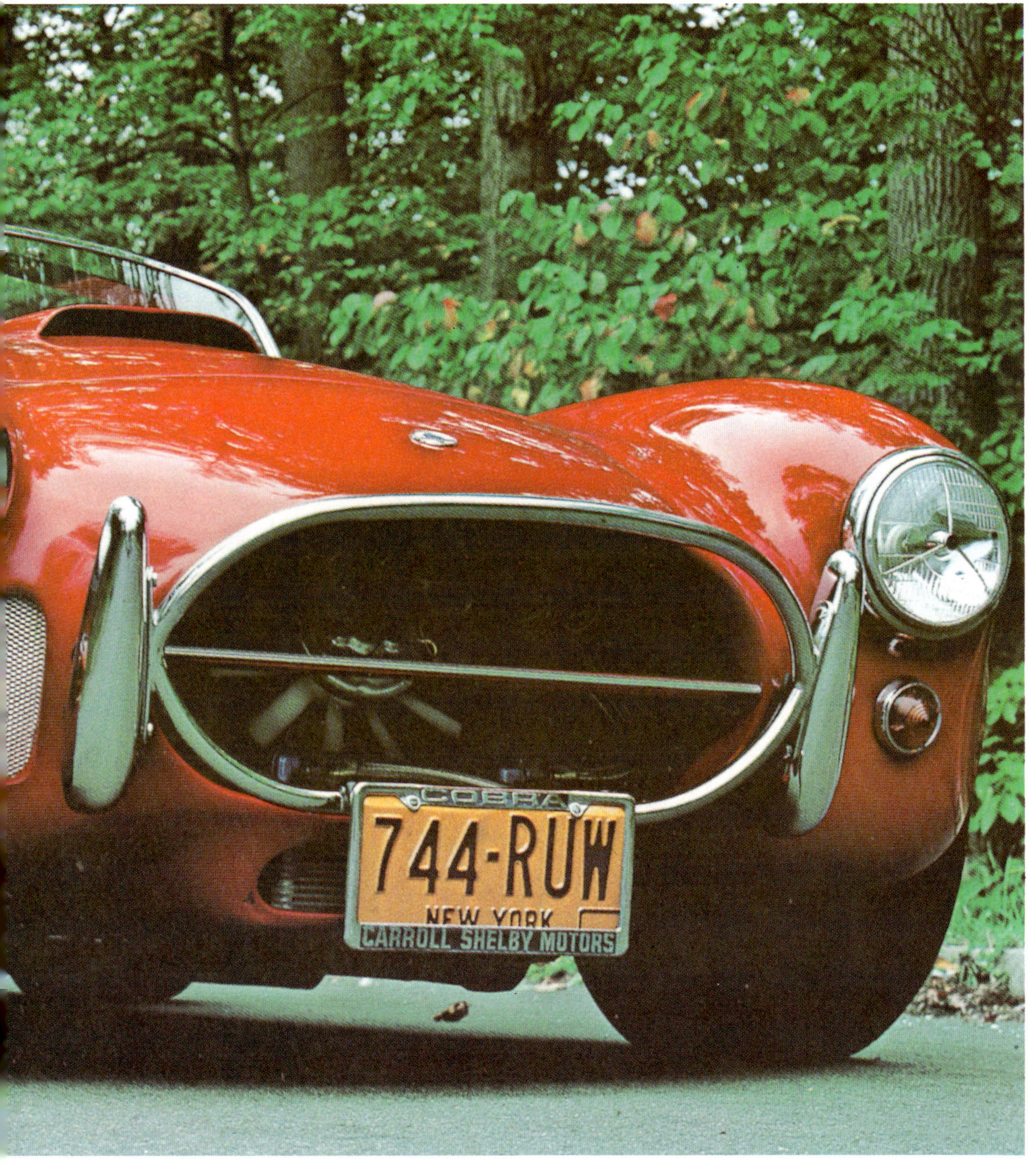
COBRA
744-RUW
NEW YORK
CARROLL SHELBY MOTORS

Above, left and right
Shelby's first colour brochure was a simple affair; the AC Cars version was a close but even simpler copy

Left *In the AC experimental department, Alan Turner stands beside the unique 1964 Le Mans Cobra, destined to be wrecked completely when a tyre burst during the race*

Right Here seen at Brands Hatch in early 1966, GPG 4C is one of the best-known British Cobras, built for Tommy Atkins in 1964 and raced by many drivers in many, many events

Below Two decades later, a laborious reconstruction of the 1964 Le Mans Cobra by Barrie Bird nears completion with panelling by the original bodybuilder, Maurice Gomm

Left *Cobras were outclassed in the US Road Racing Championship series: a 1965 paddock shot at Bridgehampton, NY, says it all*

Below *Cobras on the grid at Watkins Glen, with a GTO Ferrari (right) among the opposition*

Right John Atkins, ACOC Cobra Registrar, scored maximum possible points when he won the British Post-Historic Racing Car Championship outright in 1982

Below Driving the famous Willment Team coupé, Ansell Rothschild leads a tight pack around Woodcote in a club race at Silverstone in 1978

batches, these were old Ace wheels, fitted back-to-front if necessary to clear larger-type brakes. 'On those cars, they looked like bicycle wheels,' says Keith Judd of AC Cars.

First in the Dean Moon shop at Santa Fe Springs, later in the larger ex-Scarab premises at Venice, California, that Shelby took over from Lance Reventlow, the Cobras were checked over and the chassis cleaned up after their long journey. The bodywork being in .045 in. aluminium, shipping damage was not at all uncommon and obviously had to be made good; race cars were usually sent unpainted. When all was ready the engine/gearbox, unit was installed and the completed car tested (but not, we suspect, by Carroll Shelby in person!) so that final adjustments could be made and the whole vehicle smartened up for its first owner.

Shelby ordered the cars from AC in batches of 100 to written specifications which, of course, were altered as necessary, and naturally there were more alterations in the early days than later on. 'He didn't ever present us with a new design,' says Alan Turner. 'He'd say, "We've got problems, what can you do about it?"' One of the earliest, and most urgently in need of solution, was serious overheating with the radiators supplied by AC Cars. Often referred to nowadays as a Ford Zephyr radiator, it was in fact the Delaney-Gallay unit previously used on the AC Greyhound, and just not up to handling the heat output of an engine more than twice the size. Ever practical, Shelby sent his men out to buy Harrison alloy radiators from all the surrounding General Motors dealers. These later gave way (except in the case of race cars) to Ford's McCord radiators, which were also good but not so light in weight. Some changes were made to keep down the cost, for the Cobra was in fact a tight-budget car however custom-built it *seemed* to be. After the first two batches had been supplied, the Smiths instruments and Lucas electrics were replaced by Stewart-Warner instruments and Ford electrics. To save payment of duty, components like these were shipped in

CHAPTER TWO

Two views of the AC paint shop during Mark III production

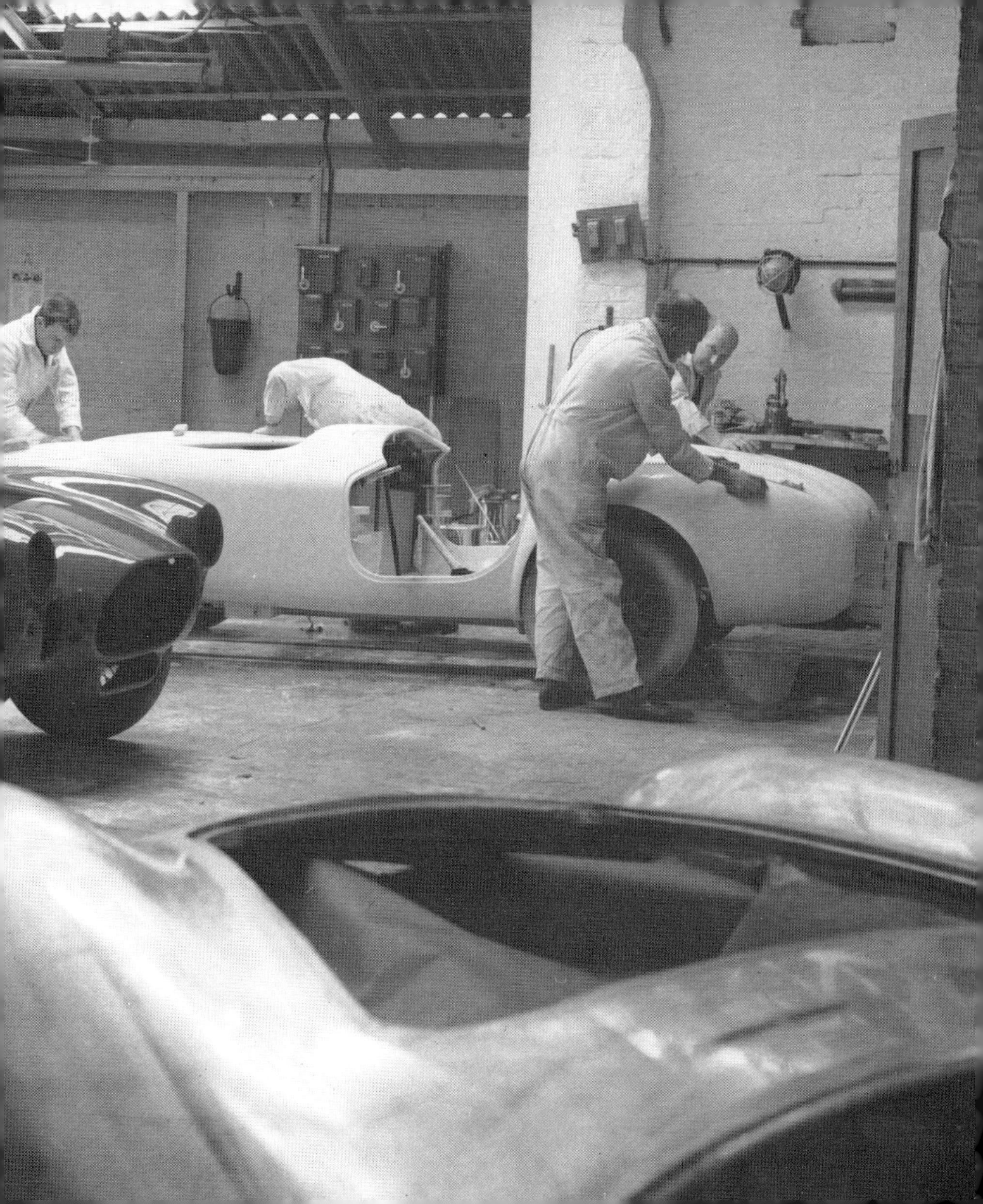

CHAPTER TWO

bulk to Britain and held in bonded stores, so that ACs could draw on them as required.

Running changes during the production life of the Cobra have been well researched and documented by the Shelby American Automobile Club in the USA, making good use of their contacts with owners in the country where most Cobras were driven and most surviving examples remain. Such changes are difficult to date exactly: customers' cars were often updated at Venice

A batch of unpainted Mark III racecars goes through at Thames Ditton, early 1965

76

after purchase, where stocks of optional components were held, and in some cases, near-identical parts were available in different forms on different sides of the Atlantic. An example of this is the bonnet intake or hood scoop on race cars. In the USA this was of fibreglass, simply pop-riveted over a hole made in the bonnet at Thames Ditton; in Europe it was of the same material as the aluminium bonnet and welded in place.

In the entire life of the Cobra only three cars were retained by Thames Ditton as factory demonstrators. The first, chassis CS-2030, was built surprisingly early on—it seems to have been in existence in September 1962, though it was not registered for road use until the beginning of November (registration number 300 PK). Keith Judd of AC Cars, who succeeded Jock Henderson as sales manager, remembers it as having always had rack-and-pinion steering, which would make it not only the first right-hand drive Cobra but also the first Mark II. It is pictured in the first British Cobra catalogue, which seems to have been produced quite a long time before right-hand drive Cobras were offered on the UK market in September 1964; Keith Judd is seen at the wheel, disguised by a touched-in pair of sunglasses, and the artist has also provided the car with side-vents. It was also well before this that the second right-hand drive Cobra, chassis COB-6004, was sold in November 1963 to a Major Parrish of the Foreign Office, who kept it quite a short time before this car, 4141 PE, passed into the hands of its present owner, Lord Cross.

The second AC demo car, also leaf-sprung, carried the next European chassis number, COB-6005, and was registered on New Year's Day 1964. As APA 6B, it remained in AC's hands for almost two years but does not seem to have been road-tested by any of the magazines; when *Autocar* published their first test report on 12 November 1965, COB-6005 had just passed on to its first private owner, and the British weekly made use of Ken Rudd's personal Mark II Cobra, CPO 681B. By that time, of course, the leaf-sprung car was in fact

CHAPTER TWO

Racecars are worked over in the brightly-lit Shelby shop at Venice, California

out of date by almost a year in the States, but not so outdated in Europe, where AC had continued to sell a trickle of Mark II models until the summer of 1965. In October 1965 the third and last demo car, COB-6106, was registered for road use as KPD 150C.

The coil-sprung chassis was fitted with a 289-cube engine, like its two predecessors, and ran on centrelock wire wheels with Dunlop HR185-15 tyres. It was eventually greeted with equal enthusiasm by *Autocar* and *Motor* when the two magazines ran road tests in 1967—but they had to call it the AC 289 Sports. Having promoted the name of Cobra until it had turned into a publicity man's dream, Shelby sold it to the Ford Motor Company, with the ironic result that although Cobra *still* meant Cobra in Europe, in the USA it was a tarted-up Ford Mustang. This was a sports car? Not hardly.

CHAPTER THREE

Beauty or beast?

To assess the qualities of a car that had its heyday 20 years ago is not easy. Tastes and standards change faster than we realize. Sampled anew, the vehicle we remember as light and responsive seems to handle like a truck, and we begin to wonder if there are any absolute standards by which a car may be judged. Perhaps there are none. We may agree with the words of A. E. Berriman: 'Today, the motorist enjoys the most luxurious mode of travel that has been devised by man.... It stands as the triumph of automobile engineering.' But would we say it of the cars that existed when he wrote those words—in 1914?

Contemporary road test reports are more reliable evidence than latter-day magazine features because the car tested is neither neglected nor over-restored. The tester judges it against the background of its own period, and the truth is not obscured by reverence or woolly romanticism—although it may have been distorted by other considerations, and performance figures sometimes have to be taken with a pinch of salt. Another and often more effective method is to talk to the men who drove the cars; preferably those who drove them fast. To race a car is to test it to the limit, and the driver is left with vivid recollections of its behaviour. It is a tough assessment, but in the case of anything worthy of the name of sports car, an entirely valid one.

Although the Tojeiro-based AC Ace was generally considered an advanced car when first announced, the man who raced it more successfully than anyone else has no illusions about it. 'That chassis wasn't rigid at all,'

CHAPTER THREE

AUTOSPORT   SEPTEMBER 4, 1964

CARS ARE PLEASED TO ANNOUNCE THAT THE RIGHT-HAND DRIVE

AC COBRA

WILL BE AVAILABLE ON THE HOME MARKET FROM SEPTEMBER 1964

Powered by Ford
4727 c.c 8-cylinder V8 engine with 4-speed all synchromesh gearbox. Price £2030 plus P.T. £424. 9s.7d. includes Heater, Demisters, Screen Wash, Wire Wheels, Bumpers front and rear (as illustrated), Tonneau Cover.

BEAUTY OR BEAST?

says Ken Rudd. 'There was nothing about it to make it successful except that it was very light, and it stuck on the ground, and it came at a time when only Lotus knew how to do things any better (towards the end, they were running us out of business). The only reason it went round corners was that the tubes were so thin, they would bend. Salvadori once tried my AC-Bristol and told me, "How you manage to drive that sort of crap, I don't know."' When we recall that the Cobra came almost a

Far left In September 1964, AC Cars announced the availability of the Cobra on the UK market at £2030 plus tax, with 289 engine—well over twice what Shelby paid for an engineless Cobra 'Courtesy of Autosport'

Above The first AC Cars Cobra for demo work, registration 300 PK

CHAPTER THREE

Above right *At the end of 1963 a new Mark II, APA 6B, took over as AC's demo car*

Below right *Third and last of AC's demo Cobras was officially an 'AC 289', with 289 engine in Mark III chassis. It is here being tested by Michael Bowler, then on the staff of* Motor

82

decade after the Ace, it is perhaps not so surprising that Denis Jenkinson made his famous remark in *Motor Sport* in 1964: 'Next time I am out in a vintage car and the inevitable peasant comes up and says, 'Ah, they don't make 'em like that nowadays', I shall say, "Oh yes they do, and they are called Cobras."'.

Cliff Davis loved his Tojeiro-Bristol, but not the Cobra: 'It was a pig—virtually undriveable.' Tony Hogg, when technical editor of *Road & Track*, defined it as 'A weapon designed specifically for proceeding from one point to another in the minimum amount of time'. He also said: 'The Cobra is a curious mixture of ancient and modern.... The suspension and steering reminded us of the cars we were driving ten years ago [i.e. 1954].... The behavior of the suspension is distinctly peculiar when the car is driven hard.... However, the effect on the roadholding is not as bad as it appears at first sight'.

CHAPTER THREE

The 289 engine installed in the Mark III chassis of KPD 150C, the last demo Cobra, as tested by Motor *magazine*

That being his opinion of the leaf-sprung Mark II, how did Hogg like the coil-sprung Mark III? Well enough, it seems, to buy one years later as a fun-car replacement for a Cadillac-engined Allard he had owned at one time. Writing of this in 1974, ten years after testing the Mark II, he said: 'Actually the car is not crude at all by 1965 standards. Admittedly it is tricky to drive hard because of the enormous power, but the suspension is excellent on good road surfaces, the brakes are superb and the steering extremely accurate. On poor surfaces the car tends to leap about and scratch for traction, and you can break traction very easily indeed when accelerating hard on any surface. There is nothing particularly treacherous about the car's basic handling qualities, because it is strictly a neutral machine.... However, the whole question is somewhat academic.... When I wrote my impression of the Allard I described it as perhaps the most dangerous car I have ever driven, but I think the Cobra surpasses it.... The trouble with the Cobra is simply its power, which is no fault at all—it's just that there is a temptation to use it'.

Frank Gardner, being a tough and outspoken Australian, recalled his Cobra racing days in blunter terms: 'They were the forerunners of the current American Can-Am type big-engined racers, and boy, did they have little going for them. Those Cobras really were animals. They bucked and skipped and crashed about, and there wasn't a lot you could do with them except keep your foot down on whatever pedal happened to be appropriate, hang on and hope. Cobras were terribly demanding cars physically, and when they started doing a crude form of triangulation on the chassis and building slippery-shaped coupé bodies, they got even hairier, if that was possible. The philosophy seemed to be that if one end didn't stick to the road you just fitted bigger tyres to it, and if it still didn't go round corners you removed the driver and bolted a new one into his place. They were difficult cars, and they were light enough, powerful enough and slippery enough to go terribly fast. And any accident you had was liable to be a bloody big one'.

Alan Mann, the man who ran the Daytona team in most of the FIA championship races of 1965, didn't agree that the cars were difficult to drive, though he did encounter other difficulties (see Chapter 4): 'The Daytonas handled so much better than the open cars that although they were heavier they were faster, even on short circuits where the aerodynamics didn't count.

What the Cobra became in the USA—a tarted-up Ford Mustang

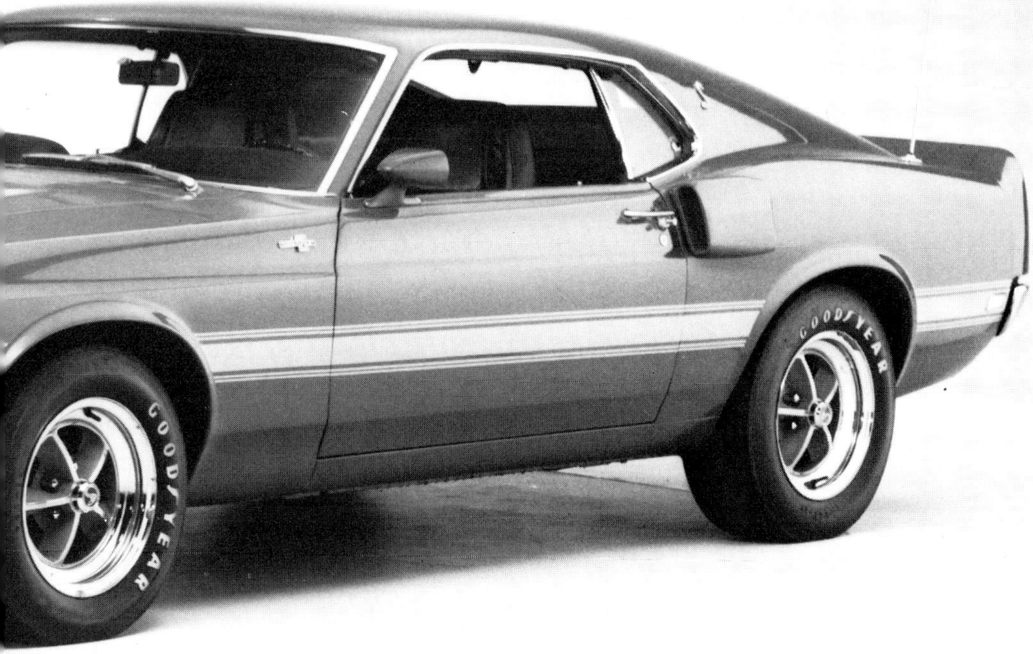
GOODYEAR
GOODYEAR

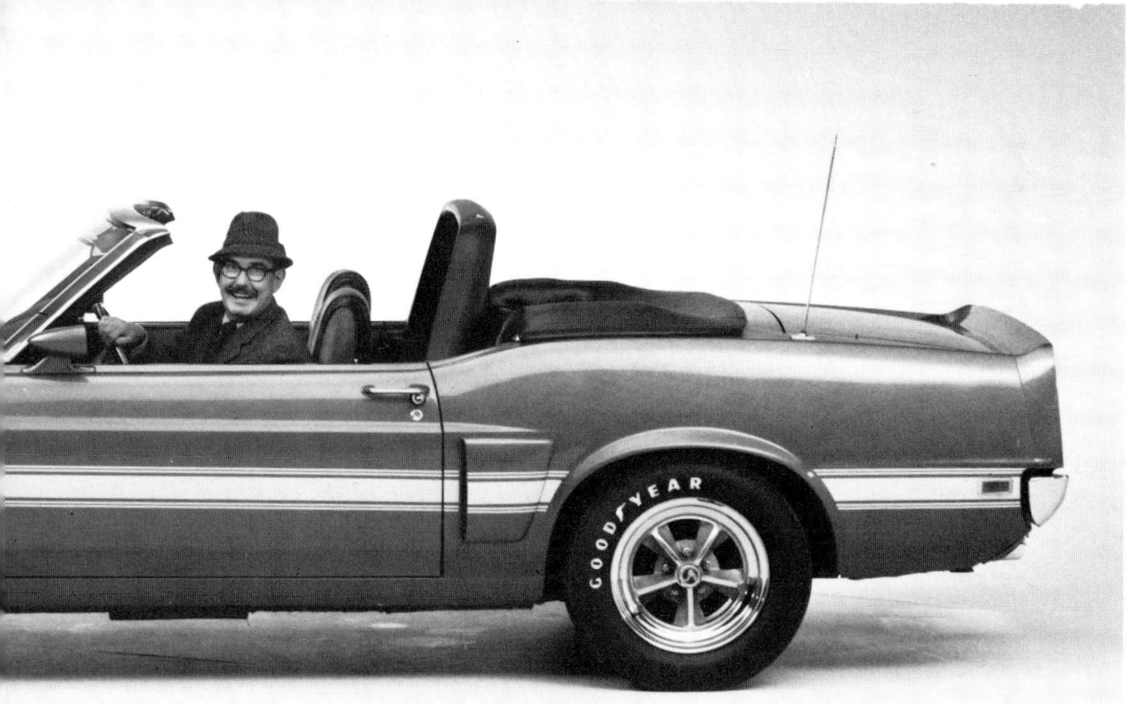
GOODYEAR

CHAPTER THREE

Those open cars were like driving a sponge around; *everything* moved. But in general the Cobras were quite easy to drive. Hard, heavy, but not difficult, because they'd slide about a lot. The directional stability was good. But no two cars were alike in any respect. And from my knowledge of what broke on the 289s, we'd have had serious problems if we'd ever tried to race the 427s'.

Jack Sears was outright winner of the British saloon car championship in 1958 and 1963, and in 1964/65 raced the Willment Racing open Cobra, AC's own 1964 coupé at Le Mans 1964, the works Daytona coupés throughout 1965, and Willment's own version of the Daytona; he is also the son of Stanley Sears, one of Britain's leading collectors of veteran and vintage machinery. In 1963 he had the choice of driving a Cobra (the Bolton/Sanderson Le Mans car of that year) or a lightweight E type Jaguar in the Tourist Trophy at Goodwood. He tried both cars in practice: 'It really was quite frightening. I'd just gone into Fordwater ahead of Mike Parkes' GTO Ferrari when this Cobra started to act like a bucking bronco, and I went sideways across the track at 100-plus, convinced I was going to have the most imperial bloody accident. In fact I did manage to hold it, but Mike had taken to the grass to avoid me, and said afterwards it was terrifying to watch—he reckoned the car must be undriveable'.

So Jack politely declined his first Cobra race, but during the winter the car was modified in the light of US racing experience, with additional mods by Jeff Uren. In 1964 he had another go at Silverstone: 'It was transformed. Suddenly it was a pleasure to drive and much more predictable, although it never handled like a GTO, and during 1964 I really made friends with that car. It gave you much more of a smack in the back than either the E type or the GTO when you put your foot down; really exciting to drive. And it could be driven hard—its handling could be forgiven. Yes, it *was* easy to drive, once it had been civilized.

'The open ones did seem to be flexing all the time—like

wringing out a towel, with one end going one way and the other end the opposite way—but the Daytona was a totally different animal. Much more rigid, more stable, and just about as fast round corners as the GTO. The Willment team's own coupé handled very well, too.

'For sheer, gutsy motoring in an almost 1930s style, really, the Cobra had it. I'd been lucky enough to do a lot of road motoring and racing in veteran and vintage sports cars—the TT Sunbeam, various Bentleys—and you know, this gave me a sympathy with the Cobra. You

Cliff Davis races LOY 500, his Tojeiro-Bristol

CHAPTER THREE

couldn't just get into one and belt it around, like a GTO; it had to be tamed like a stallion, or some wild woman. Today's racing drivers would be appalled by the way a typical Cobra behaved. But it was a car of enormous character.'

As mentioned earlier, there is much rivalry between champions of the leaf-sprung and coil-sprung cars—and in Europe, where both variants are to be found, between owners of Mark III Cobras with small or big engines. The last Cobra of all was bought by an English engineer, Ian Richardson, who raced it very successfully with a 289 engine extensively modified ('You had to mod those engines a lot so's they'd take some wellie') and liked the combination of small engine and coil-sprung chassis. 'My old car was quite fast, for a Cobra—they were never *really* fast on corners or you were into the Kamikaze brigade—and the trick was not to pull the suspension up hard. There was no give in that massive chassis frame, designed for the 7-litre engine, and it went absolutely wild if you made it too tight; we used stock road springs, adjustable shockers, and just a very thin anti-roll bar on the back to give a *little* bit of control. It was a horrible car, really, that kind of grew on you—I had my best days of racing with it, and five circuit records in one year. It was well-balanced, too, with the 289 engine, but not with that bloody great 7-litre shoved in.'

Barrie Bird, on the other hand, prefers the earlier chassis and respects the historical continuity to be found in the transverse-leaf series. 'My personal opinion is this: the Mark I and Mark II chassis worked, as did the Ace before them and Cliff Davis' Tojeiro before that. If you study the geometry, even by the technology of the 1950s it shouldn't have worked as well, but it did. The reason it did was that the chassis frame provided part, the major part, of the suspension. That wasn't luck or chance. Thames Ditton goes back to 1903, and virtually all of their cars were flexible, following the 1920s/1930s technology of pretty stiff suspension and a fairly flexible frame joining it together. AC Cars understood very well

BEAUTY OR BEAST?

Courtesy of Eileen Brockbank

Below *Stirling Moss* (centre, bearded) *managed the* Sunday Times *sponsored entry of a Cobra which came 10th overall at Le Mans in 1963; the Shelby-entered Cobra did not finish the race*

CHAPTER THREE

Another view of the Sanderson/Bolton AC Cobra, with its distinctive long hardtop, at Le Mans 1963

that the frame was a lifed item, and when a car came into Service Department they would expect, look for and correct fatigue cracks in the main chassis. You may not like it by modern standards, but that's how it was done.

'Then along comes Ford, a huge outfit with an entirely different attitude: the old hands who would have understood this philosophy probably all disappeared in the 1940s, and the college boys who had come to the top in the 1960s believed in modern technology. That means coil springs and shockers just like a Grand Prix car, just like Colin Chapman was designing, and leaf springs are anathema. So Thames Ditton comes in for a lot of push to modernize things, and the opportunity comes with the inevitable American decision to use the 'bigger, better' 7-litre engine. Talk to American Cobra enthusiasts nowadays, they're very much switched into the big-engined cars and the small ones have far less status. You can point out that it's the smaller-engined, leaf-sprung cars that still win the races, and they just produce the standing-quarter acceleration figures.

'I think the two prongs of the change were the engineering staff's desire to 'improve' things, and the customers' belief that if 289 cubic inches were good, 427 cubic inches must be better. Alan Turner of ACs knew that the coil spring design would be a disaster with a flexible chassis, but he had to retain the ladder frame to make the change quickly, so he did his best by going up in tube size, making it a bit stiffer but not much. Although in theory the Mark III should be better, in practice it isn't—they're no faster around a corner than a Mark II. Also they are heavier, more unwieldy, and the only place where the Marks III Cobras were successful was on a somewhat artificial circuit like Daytona where a good driver could push one up to 200 mph. Everywhere else, they didn't match up to the earlier cars.'

It might be thought that contemporary road test reports would settle the question, but Cobra road tests are a pretty strange collection, with quoted performance figures that look suspiciously like estimates, guesswork or plain wishful thinking. One of the strangest, in its way, was the first *Road & Track* test of what they called the 'AC-Ford Cobra', published in the issue of September 1962 and used as the basis of the Cobra catalogue on both sides of the Atlantic. This car, we were told, achieved 7000 rpm in top—153 mph on the 3.54:1 ratio fitted,

Later acquired by Willment and raced as an open car, the 1963 Le Mans Cobra was at first 'quite frightening' to Jack Sears, but in 1964 he enjoyed racing it. Here he holds off Chris Amon to place 5th overall in the Guards Trophy at Brands Hatch after a heart-stopping duel throughout the race

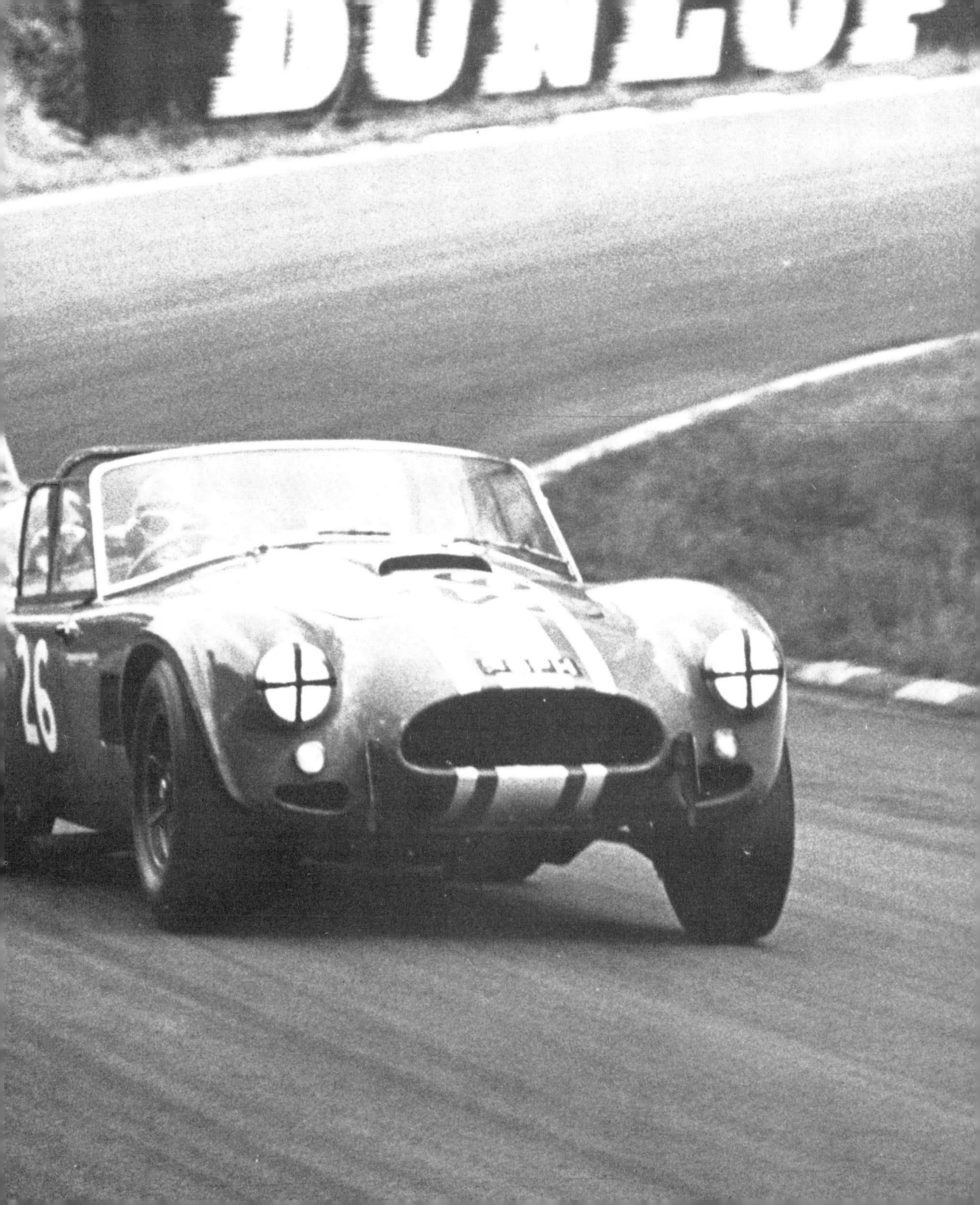
26

CHAPTER THREE

Phil Remington (standing centre, facing camera) supervises the testing of a Mark III racecar at Silverstone. Far right is Alan Turner

giving 21.8 mph per 1000 rpm—and did the standing quarter-mile in 13.8 secs *with a 'street' 260-cube engine*, which was described as 'virtually stock Ford but equipped with solid valve lifters and a camshaft of non-standard but unspecified timing'. This remarkable engine, advertised as giving 260 bhp at 5800 rpm, would apparently run up to 7200 rpm without distress or significant power fall-off. We were told that the Cobra would reach 40, 60, 80 and 100 mph in, respectively, 2.5, 4.2, 6.8 and 10.8 secs when tested at Riverside Raceway,

BEAUTY OR BEAST?

The last Cobra (or 'AC 289', as it had become) leaves the line at Thames Ditton, 7 December 1968. On the right a batch of Frua 428 convertibles—successor to the Cobra—begins to take shape

'which has enough straightaway room to allow the Cobra to reach its top speed, but not enough to permit timing the car over a measured distance at that speed'. The highly impressive figure of 153 mph was not, therefore, the result of averaging two or more timed runs in opposite directions to nullify the effect of wind speed, but the interpretation of a one-way reading on the tachometer.

The claimed 153 mph very soon became 155 in Shelby literature, but it didn't stop there, rising to a figure of 175 mph which was quoted in motor magazines in both the UK and the USA. And this was still with the 260/260 engine! The Cobra myth was nicely launched on its way. Even with a tuned 289 engine giving around 330 bhp on four double-choke Webers, a special 3.07:1 final drive and an equally special hardtop, the Cobra which finished seventh overall in the 1963 Le Mans race was timed at no more than 160 mph on the Mulsanne straight. The same car, with final drive changed to 3.77, was timed at 139.6 mph on the banked MIRA test circuit by *Motor*'s Eric Dymock, who reckoned he might have got it wound up to about 148 on a longer straight. His quoted time for the standing quarter, however, was a rather extraordinary

Two views of John Woolfe's ex-Feutel Mark III, repatriated from the USA, converted to rhd and tested by Motor *in 1967. It reached 100 mph from rest in 9.8 sec.*

CHAPTER THREE

11 secs—even more extraordinary for a car which had not been given so much as an oil-change after maintaining well over 100 mph for the full twenty-four hours of Le Mans.

Some weeks before this *Motor* test, *Autosport* had published one of a 289-engined Mark II with 'QQ' temporary registration which was said to be Shelby's personal Cobra. This, too, had the 3.77:1 ratio now standardized, so the timed maximum speed of 136 mph quoted by John Bolster sounded reasonable, but one might have expected better acceleration figures than *Road & Track* had claimed with a 260 engine and 3.54 ratio. Not so. Bolster's times were 5.2, 8.2 and 13.0 secs to 60, 80 and 100 mph, though he quoted exactly the same time as *Road & Track*—13.8 secs—for the standing quarter.

A year later, in June 1964, *Road & Track* got around to publishing a test report of a Mark II with 289/271 'street' engine, its modifications including high-lift camshafts, bigger valves, single four-choke carburettor, solid lifters and a compression ratio of 11.6:1. Written by Tony Hogg, whose comments on the car were quoted earlier in this chapter, it was a very different affair from the magazine's original Cobra test, and the performance figures were very much more believable: a maximum speed of 139 mph at 6900 rpm, the standing quarter in 14 secs dead, and acceleration to 40, 60, 80 and 100 mph in 3.4, 6.6, 10.8 and 14.1 secs.

In Britain it was still difficult to secure a Cobra for road test, and the one that *Autocar* tried towards the end of 1965 was, in fact, Ken Rudd's personal Cobra—still a Mark II although they were out of production by then. As Tony Hogg had remarked that the Cobra seemed undergeared to him, it is interesting to see that Rudd's had retained the earlier 3.54 ratio. Moreover, for their high-speed test *Autocar* fitted Dunlop Racing tyres which raised the gearing another 10 per cent to give 23.8 mph per 1000 rpm. Their timed maximum of 138 mph was therefore achieved at a mere 5800 rpm, and they

Powerhouse of John Woolfe's 427 Mark III

reckoned the car was now slightly overgeared—that it would, perhaps, have topped a genuine 140 mph on lower overall gearing. But the testers found it an interesting enough experience: 'Above about 80 mph the fabric hood [top] billows taut like a drum-skin and pulls its edges clear of the sidescreens. After a mile or two at maximum speed we noticed the screen rail had lifted off the glass along its top edge.... At these three-figure speeds there is a tremendous roar of wind noise.... Conversation is impossible, and we had to communicate by hand signs and lip-reading.'

On standard tyres and despite the 3.54 back end, they recorded 'the steepest acceleration curve we have ever plotted', with a standing quarter in 13.9 secs and speeds of 40, 60, 80 and 100 mph reached in 3.2, 5.5, 8.9 and 14.0 secs. They had not equalled John Bolster's figures with

CHAPTER THREE

the 3.77 axle, but certainly came close to them, and commented mildly that the acceleration was 'sensational—very similar to taking off in a piston-engined aircraft with an open cockpit.'

Two years later, *Motor* sampled a Mark III, but it was the car now marketed in Europe as the 'AC 289', with 289/271 engine installed in a coil-sprung chassis. The quoted kerb weight was little different—2352 lb instead of 2315—and the overall gearing was 21.5 mph per 1000 rpm, but for some reason the mean maximum (timed on Continental roads) was just 134.9 mph, described as 'ear-shattering' at 6300 rpm. It was noted, however, that this speed might be slightly improved with the 3.31:1 final drive which was to be standardized in Europe. Acceleration was almost identical to that recorded by *Motor*'s sister magazine, with the anomaly that although the standing quarter was appreciably slower at 14.4 secs, the magic 100 mph was reached in only 13.7 secs, making it 'the fastest car to 100 mph that we have tested, by just 0.1 sec from the TVR Tuscan with the same engine'.

Would the Mark III Cobra have proved a whole lot faster with 427 engine in genuine timed tests? It is difficult to say. So many so-called 427 Cobras were in reality fitted with the much softer 428 engine. So few of them got to Europe. And the most responsible US magazine, *Road & Track*, never tested a 427-engined Mark III while it was a production model.

A retrospective test feature by Tony Hogg was published in a 1974 issue of the magazine, but most of the quoted performance figures were merely estimated or calculated. So far as acceleration was concerned, these differed little at the bottom end from those recorded by *Autocar* and *Motor* with the 289 engine: 3.3 secs to 40, 5.3 to 60, and a leisurely 9.4 to 80 mph. The standing quarter was given as a more impressive 13.8 secs, accompanied by an even 13 secs to 100 mph—but these, after all, were the self-same times that Bolster had claimed for a 289-engined Mark II as early as 1963. Maximum speed was a different story. Tony Hogg suggested 162 mph at

6500 rpm, signifying a surprisingly high overall gearing of 25 mph per 1000 rpm for a car that was said to have a 3.54 final drive; the overall gearing for another Mark III with 3.31 axle worked out at 26 mph per 1000. On this basis, incidentally, Dick Smith's remarkable Mark III was reaching some 7600 rpm when timed at 198 mph at Daytona.

One 427-engined Mark III that made it to Europe was, in fact, one of a pair originally sold to Ed Feutel for road work and racing, with engines reputedly giving 500 and 550 bhp, and converted to rhd by John Woolfe, who brought the cars to England. Roger Bell of *Motor* borrowed the road-equipped machine, which he described as 'the world's easiest car to spin around the gearlever on a wet road' despite Firestone Grand Prix tyres of 12.00 in. section on the rear and 9.20 in. on the front. Restricted to a MIRA speed test, he was unable to approach the theoretical maximum of 165 mph at 7000 rpm, but he was timed electronically at 148.8 and just managed to see 153 mph before running out of room—exactly the speed, be it noted, that *Road & Track* had claimed five years earlier for a Mark I Cobra with a 'street' 260/260 Ford Fairlane engine . . . . The acceleration figures, too, bore a close resemblance, with 2.6, 4.2 and 6.8 secs to 40, 60 and 80 mph, but his standing quarter was achieved in 12.4 secs and his 0 to 100 mph time of 9.8 secs went into the *Guinness Book of Records* as the fastest by a production car—if the extensively tweaked Woolfe Cobra could be called a production car. It was this same vehicle, by the way, which Michael Bowler (later editor of *Thoroughbred and Classic Cars*) remembers as 'the only car on which I have run out of fuel twice within 10 miles'.

But it seems that the ultimate Cobra was built for— who else?—Carroll Shelby, according to a test report published in *Road & Track* in February 1968. The much-chromed 427 engine was fitted with two Paxton superchargers working in parallel at about 6 psi, each feeding a four-barrel Holley, with a 3-speed Ford T6

CHAPTER THREE

With the Brooklands banking in the background, Brian Angliss poses alongside his brainchild, the Autokraft replica Cobra of 1984

automatic transmission and a 3.31:1 final drive. Shelby claimed 800 bhp, which is perhaps as credible as most of the figures he quoted, but *Road & Track* did find it impossible to hold the car on its brakes while trying to rev the engine up to torque coverter stall speed. So the auto transmission was allowed to do its own shifting at 6200 rpm, and apparently did so without wheelspin. Electronically timed at Orange County Raceway, the twin-blown Shelby Cobra recorded 2.6, 3.8, 5.6 and 7.9 secs to 40, 60, 80 and 100 mph, and the standing quarter time was 11.9 secs with a terminal speed of 116. A maximum speed test was not attempted; theoretically, it would have been 182 mph at 7000 rpm, but if you can reach 75 in first gear and 126 in second, who needs top gear?

CHAPTER FOUR

Championship year

The championship title that the Cobra is popularly thought to have won in 1965, the FIA *Championnat du Monde des Constructeurs*, ceased to exist some six months before the first Cobra was built. Shelby and Ford laid on such a stupendous publicity exercise (in which, as *Newsweek* shrewdly remarked at the time, 'Both carefully play down AC's role') that few Americans can have realized this. But that's how it was.

It happened this way. Back in 1953 it started as a contest between sports car manufacturers in the world's seven major sports car races: the Sebring 12 Hours, Mille Miglia, Le Mans 24 Hours, Belgian 24 Hours, Nürburgring 1000 Kilometres, the Tourist Trophy in Ulster and the Carrera Panamericana in Mexico. The prestige of such a title, known in English-speaking countries as the World Sports Car Championship, was beyond all question. Though the qualifying events and cars changed from time to time by FIA edict, they were great races and great cars—Alfa Romeo, Aston Martin, Cunningham, Ferrari, Jaguar, Lancia, Lotus, Maserati, Osca, Porsche—handled by the cream of the world's drivers.

Unfortunately the cars became so specialized and costly that many manufacturers dropped out— particularly as Ferrari took the title seven times in nine years. In 1961 this classic series ended, replaced for 1962 by what *Autocourse* called 'a series of ill-defined championships'—no less than five titles altogether, and a mixed bag of sixteen qualifying races. With all prestige gone from the contest, the better drivers and manufac-

Pete Brock (right) and helpers plan the body shape of the first Daytona coupé, late 1963 in California

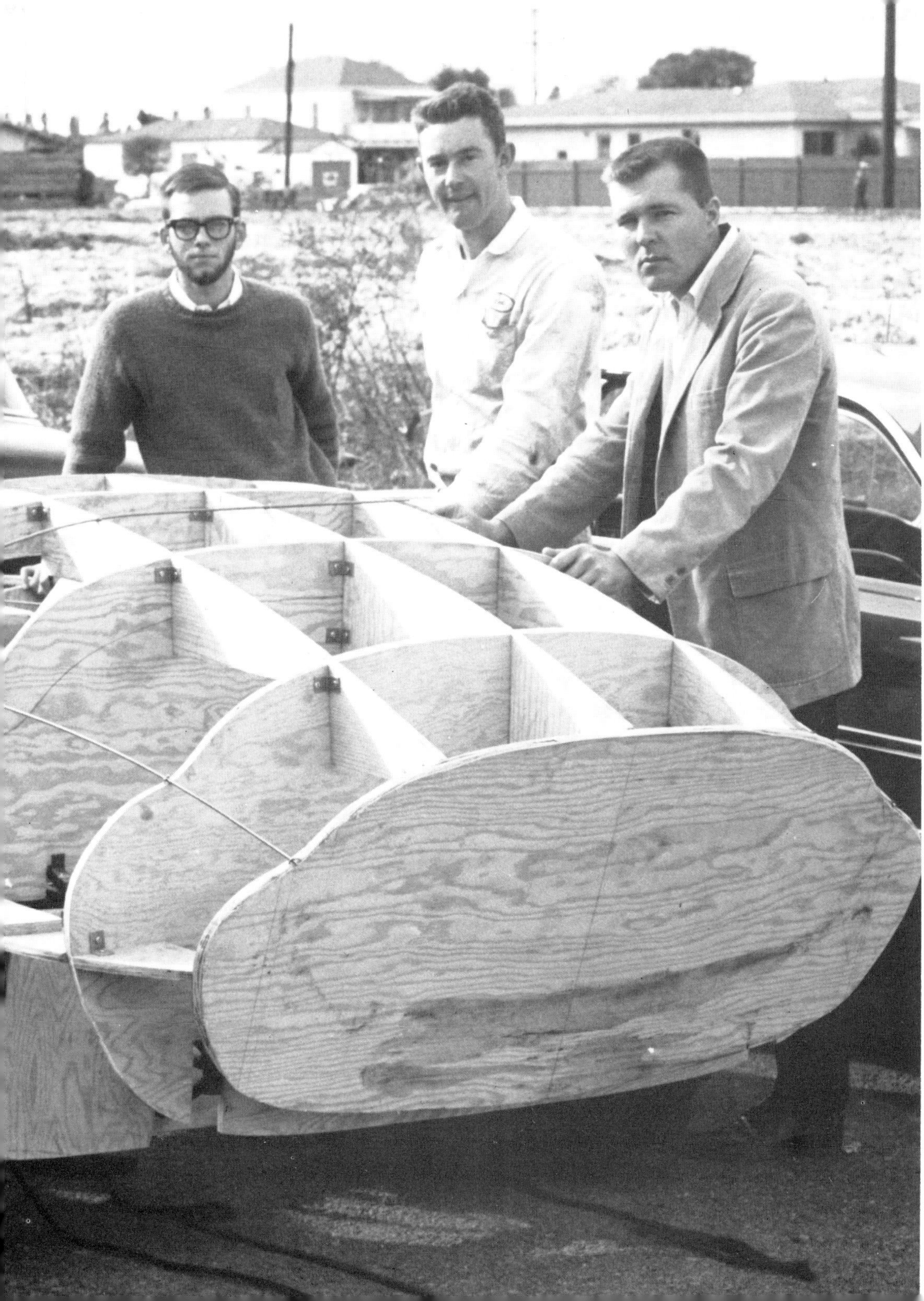

CHAPTER FOUR

Things begin to turn into reality in the body shop at California Metal Shaping

turers didn't want to know any more, and it proved just as unpopular with race organizers because the spectators weren't interested either. Some of the events were incorporated in classic races, others held separately, and the drivers who took part were second-string names in cars that were often privately owned and prepared. Predictably, Ferrari continued to dominate the *Coupe Sport* (for sports/racing cars), the *Challenge Mondial* (for

GT prototypes) and the GT Championship Division III (over 2000 cc), while Division I (up to 1000 cc) and Division II (up to 2000 cc) were invariably won by Abarth and Porsche. When a qualifying event formed part of a major sports car race, it was rare for the highest-placed GT finisher to figure in the first three.

The advent of Pete Brock's splendid Daytona coupé made the otherwise outdated Cobra a more competitive

Tryout time for the barely-finished coupé at Riverside Raceway: it's early February 1964 but this is California, and shirt-off weather for a busy man

CHAPTER FOUR

Above right The first Daytona, now with a name, arrives at the Le Mans test day in April 1964

Below right In no sense a copy of the Pete Brock coupé (as some have said), AC's own racing coupé was designed by Alan Turner. Here it is seen in the experimental shop at Thames Ditton, early 1964

machine in European racing during 1964, when despite many mechanical failures the team gained enough points to place third behind Ferrari and Porsche in the GT prototype contest. In 1965 it was decided by Ford Division—not Shelby American—that GT Division III was a sitting duck for the Cobras. Denied FIA homologation for both the 250LM *and* the 275GTB, Enzo Ferrari had not surprisingly pulled out of the category altogether. With just one privately-entered GTO running at Daytona and none at all at Sebring, the Cobras had little difficulty in amassing a 24-point lead in the first two qualifying events of the season, and it was at Florida that the decision was taken to go for the championship. In reaching it, Ford were influenced by

CHAPTER FOUR

the availability of one quiet-spoken Englishman, who could scarcely have been more different from Carroll Shelby.

Alan Mann had run a successful racing team for a British Ford dealer and met John Holman when competing with a Cortina GT at the Marlboro 12 Hours. Moreover he had helped sort out the works Falcon rally cars to such good effect that eight of them all reached the finish of the 1964 Monte, one in second place overall. At Ford's request, he had also run a development programme on the Mustang which started before that model was made public, and prepared two cars which came first and second in the GT category of the Tour de France that same year. Ford Division now asked Mann to take over the Cobra team cars for the remainder of the 1965 season, acting as an independent contractor (he had already declined the offer of a fulltime Ford job because 'the politics were too strong for me').

There were eleven more championship events to come, and the first of them was the Monza 1000 Kilometres on 25 April. 'We had a month to get used to the idea—which was a long time, by Ford standards! But it wasn't difficult, really, because we're talking about cars we never changed spring rates on, anti-roll bars, never attempted any real chassis tuning because it was such an impossible chassis to do anything with. It really was *so* bad. At Monza, for instance, I checked that we had three inches' clearance for the front wheels at full bump, and yet in the race, on the banking, the tyres were blistering the bodywork! It's impossible to fine-tune the suspension on a chassis like that because you don't know what the hell's happening. If it worked you left the thing alone. On a car like the Cobra you could make what *looked* like an improvement and screw it up completely.

'The Daytonas were a lot quicker than the open cars, with that great space-frame on top of the chassis. It was fortunate that homologation was a whole lot easier when the coupé was accepted: the rules said you couldn't alter the chassis, but you could modify it to take the

Teatime at Le Mans, 1964. Left to right are Derek Hurlock and drivers Sears and Bolton; behind, the elegant Turner coupé and AC's far from elegant ragtop Bedford truck

CHAMPIONSHIP YEAR

CHAPTER FOUR

Another shot of AC's Cobra coupé at Le Mans 1964—its only race, for the car was wrecked completely when a rear tyre burst during the night, and Peter Bolton escaped death by a miracle

closed bodywork. So, officially, all that extra bracing was only there to hold the body on! Shelby shipped the cars to me after Sebring, just as they were; I think we had an open car and all the coupés. And we took on one of his English mechanics, Charlie Agapiou. All we had to do with those cars was just keep them reliable—our only competition was the GTO Ferrari and we could run quicker than the GTOs, except maybe at Nürburgring. We didn't care if the Porsche 904s beat us sometimes because they were only in the 2-litre class; my brief was to win a specific championship, not go looking for glory on the racing circuits, so if the Porsches gave us competition we didn't argue with them. We almost never drove the Cobras hard, and sometimes we drove them extremely slowly to make sure of winning our own class.

Racing, from where I sit on the pit-counter, should be as boring as possible! Don't forget that Enzo Ferrari wasn't even looking in our direction that year—if we'd been faced by a serious Ferrari factory effort we wouldn't have known what hit us.

'So the only thing we needed to do with the Cobra was make sure we threw everything away after each race—and I mean *everything*: engine, transmission, chassis components, the lot. I had duplicate cars everywhere so that as one pair were being raced the other two were being rebuilt. The uprights used to go, so we fitted new uprights. The hub bearing housings used to expand, so we threw them away. We scrapped the engine after every race—didn't even take the heads off to look inside. It was a lousy engine, the 289, and basically unreliable, though $250,000-worth of development would have made it a world-beater. Badly built; we used to strip out the bottom end when they arrived from Shelby and have them rebuilt by Stuart Mathieson, but we still had to keep them down to about 6500 rpm at the most. The bodies weren't too bad, for aluminium, but they cracked a lot because the Italians make 'em quick, with a bag and a hammer, instead of wheeling them. And no two were ever the same; you couldn't take the windscreen from one car and use it in another.

'I was on cost-plus, with a Ford accountant coming in every couple of months to check how many man-hours we'd worked, how many air tickets we'd bought. I employed the drivers, race by race, and because we started so late in the season I had to take whoever was available of the right quality. I would put a local driver in the team if he was a good chap, competent, and did what he was told: Jo Schlesser in France, Jochen Neerpasch in Germany. But I had to keep Ford Division happy, and they always wanted an American driver to win. So, as far as drivers were concerned, all the results were fixed. Look at the practice times if you don't believe me. Bondurant didn't have the experience of Sears and Whitmore, but we needed an American driver to win

CHAPTER FOUR

CHAMPIONSHIP YEAR

because they could get more publicity in the States out of a win by an American than some unknown European. I could never *tell* my European drivers this, but I knew they would take their orders without asking questions. As you know, that's how we operate; we expect a guy to do precisely what he's told during a race.'

But there was a problem the first time out, at Monza. Alan Mann could never be sure which tyre would give the best results at a particular track, but fortunately he was free to experiment between makes because Dearborn had decreed that he was to operate on a Ford-only budget, without bonus payments from accessory people or anyone else. At Monza, a circuit that tended to be hard on tyres, he ran the Bondurant/Grant car on Goodyears and the Sears/Whitmore one on Firestones, keeping the two Cobras trundling safely around at the head of the over-2000 cc class although one of the smaller

Above *John Whitmore, the other British driver in the Cobra team. Though he preferred to forget his title, he was invariably 'Sir John' to the Americans*

Above left *'Gentleman Jack' Sears, one of the two leading British drivers in the Cobra championship team*

Far left *Alan Mann, architect of the Cobra's GT championship success in 1965; he managed the team cars and drivers in all European events*

117

CHAPTER FOUR

Right *Australian Frank Gardner drives the Willment team's copy of the Daytona coupé in the 1965 TT at Oulton Park, England*

Below *Another TT shot, with John Whitmore tailing Allen Grant*

118

Porsches, leading the under-2000 cc class, was well in front. Late in the race Bondurant suddenly speeded up, ignoring pit signals. According to Mann, he discovered afterwards that Shelby had made a private arangement with the two Americans to ensure that the Goodyear-shod car won the class. The result was an ultimatum from Alan Mann to Ford Division: if Shelby attended any more championship events in Europe, the Cobras would not start. Except at Le Mans, he never appeared again.

On home ground for the Tourist Trophy at Oulton Park, Mann entered John Whitmore with an open Cobra and Jack Sears with a closed one. There were half-a-dozen other Cobras in the race, opposed by one privately owned GTO Ferrari driven by Peter Sutcliffe, but in the first of the two two-hour heats Sutcliffe ran through non-stop to win the GT category. Sears had brake trouble, Whitmore needed to stop for tyres and fuel, and was almost asphyxiated by a leaking exhaust. Mann whipped him off to the medical centre for oxygen treatment before the second race, and decided to try running non-stop this time. So Sutcliffe sat behind Whitmore for most of the second heat, waiting to take the lead when the Cobra refuelled, and confident of a class-win when he saw

119

CHAPTER FOUR

Mann give the come-in signal. But the signal was a fake, and by the time Sutcliffe realized he'd been fooled, it was too late to catch the Cobra. Whitmore finished ahead of the Ferrari, Allen Grant just behind, followed by Sears and the rest of the Cobra drivers. It was a near thing, for Whitmore's car had a bald left rear tyre and ran out of juice on the closing-down lap.

The next round of the championship was the Targa Florio, but as five Cobras had fallen apart on the famous Sicilian mountain circuit the previous year, Alan Mann gave it a miss to concentrate on Spa the following week. In the Targa, Bondurant and Whitmore shared a Ford GT40 which retired, and the over-2000 cc GT class went to a GTO Ferrari. A Ferrari pulled it off again in Belgium, Sutcliffe getting his revenge by finishing fourth overall ahead of Bondurant to win the class, although both were beaten by Ben Pon's Porsche 904 which had also won the GT category at Monza. John Whitmore, well placed in the early stages, bounced off another car and wrecked the front end of his Cobra. But with six races run, Cobra still led Ferrari by 60.0 points to 43.9.

Whitmore returned to a GT40 for the Nürburgring race, but the works Ferraris whacked the Fords in the main event, as they had at Monza and in Sicily. Bondurant went well to take the GT category outright, partnered by Neerpasch and finishing seventh overall, while Sears and Frank Gardner came tenth overall for a class second—an experience that Gardner seemingly didn't enjoy. 'After the race, it took two days for our wrists to go down after fighting the kickback from that steering. Believe me, any normal saloon car would go round corners better than they did.'

Three weeks later but still in Germany came the Rossfeld hillclimb, close to Hitler's favourite country retreat outside Berchtesgaden, which American troops had captured almost exactly 20 years before. Short of open cars, Mann gave the factory Cobra to Bondurant and invited Bo Ljungfeldt, the Swedish rally champion, to drive another Cobra which was in fact a stock roadgoing machine owned by *Autosport* correspondent Patrick McNally, but fitted with a different engine. It was not an arrangement to Bondurant's liking, and he complained afterwards in a *Road & Track* article that he had been given a dud car. That isn't how Alan Mann remembers it: Bob had the better car by a long way, but he didn't realize the kind of driver that funny-looking, half-bald Swede was. He was really pissed off.' Nevertheless, the class-win went to Bondurant, who made two climbs within one-fifth of a second of each other, for the results were based on aggregate times, and Ljungfeldt's first timed run was a slow one. Both Cobras were well and truly beaten by Müller's Porsche 904, which set a new GT record, but as he was running in the 2-litre class it didn't matter.

Next came Le Mans, which was an almost unmitigated disaster for all the Ford entries. The entry had been decided early in the year, before the decision to go for the GT championship, and Alan Mann had to take over the AC Cars Ltd and Ford France entries, which he allocated to Jack Sears and an American dentist, Dick Thompson, plus Jo Schlesser with another American driver, Allen Grant. Jerry Grant was sharing a Shelby-entered Cobra with Dan Gurney, and Bob Johnson was paired with Tom Payne, his Daytona and Sebring partner, in another Shelby entry. Whitmore, Bondurant and others were driving GT40s, this being the great beat-hell-out-of-Ferrari year except that it didn't work out that way. The Ford challenge came to pieces as one car after another fell apart, giving the Ferraris an easy 1-2-3 victory *and* the GT category because the third-placed GTB had just been homologated, while the fifth-placed Porsche 904 rubbed it in by taking the 2-litre GT class.

After more than twelve hours' racing the only Cobra still around was the Sears/Thompson car, which had had two quite impressive crashes and could not accelerate for more than six or seven seconds without losing all oil pressure. Thoroughly fed-up, Sears wanted to retire, and

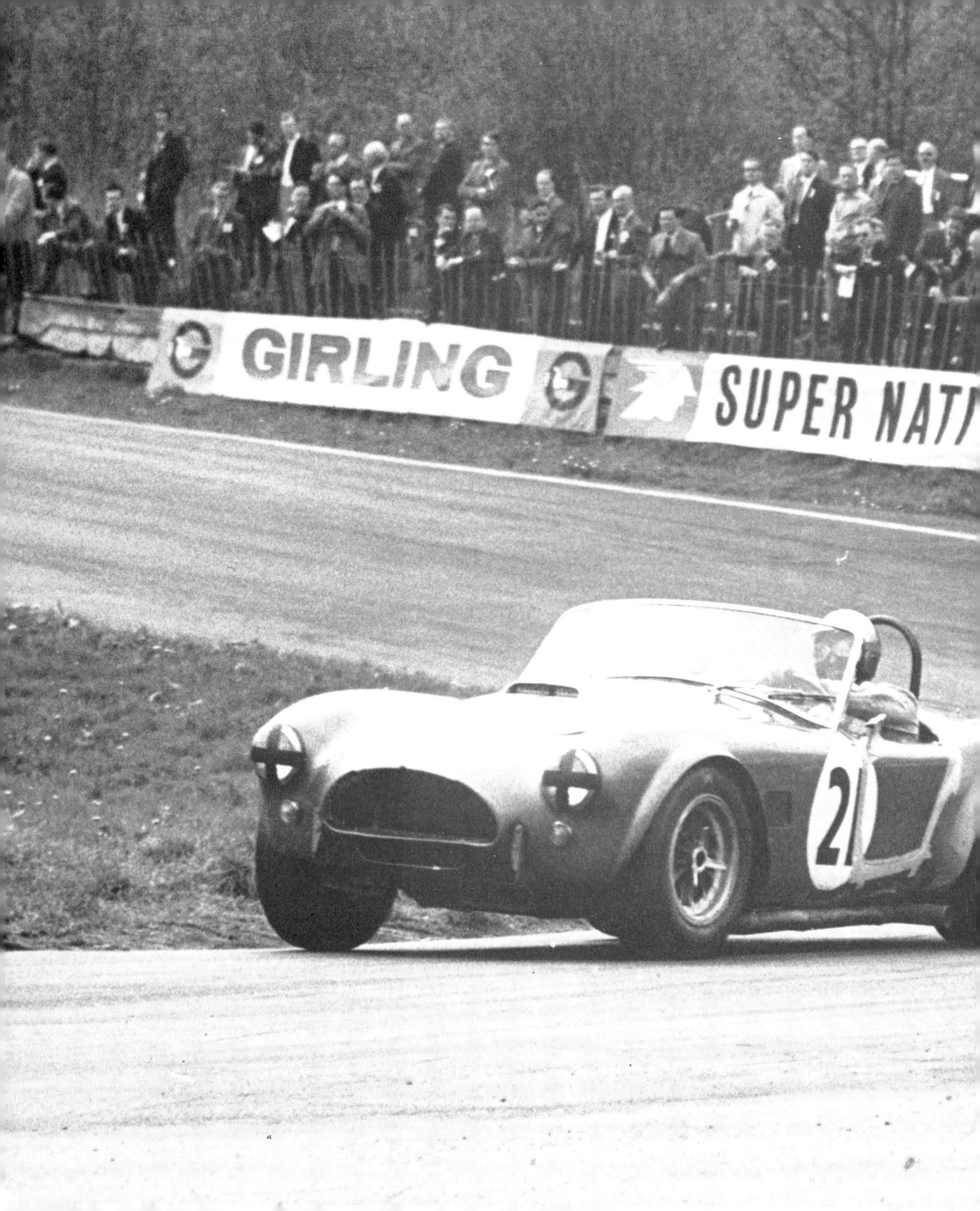
GIRLING
SUPER NAT
21

In the second heat of the 1965 TT, Whitmore holds off Sutcliffe's 250 GTO/64 Ferrari to finish 4th overall and first in the GT category

CHAPTER FOUR

In the Nürburgring 1000 Kilometres, the Daytona of Bondurant and Neerpasch goes well to finish 7th overall, once again winning the GT category for Cobra

there ensued a full, frank and meaningful discussion behind the pits. 'This is pointless,' said Gentleman Jack. 'But we've *got* to try and finish one Ford at least,' said Alan Mann. 'You can do it—just drive the bloody thing on its oil pressure.' 'I totally disagree with you,' said Sears, 'But of course I'll do what you say.' And he did. 'He could have blown it on Mulsanne any time,' says Mann. 'But he just sat there doing what he was told for the rest of the race. Now *that* is discipline!' So although the Ferrari GTB won the class, Sears and Thompson finished eighth overall to secure for Cobra a valuable 12 points for second place in the over-2000 cc GT class.

With four championship events still to go, the position was that Cobra had a lead of 28.7 points but Ferrari could still win, in the unlikely situation of the Cobras

CHAMPIONSHIP YEAR

Le Mans 1965 was a bad time for Cobras. The Sears/Thompson car, here seen leading Shelby's Johnson/Payne entry, was the only one to last the race. It came 8th overall, 2nd in class

scoring no more points and the Ferraris winning every time, for some events rated more points than others and the ones that counted were the best seven by each entrant, taking six races and one hillclimb.

At Reims on 3/4 July the only works Ferraris entered for the 12 Hours were prototypes (which filled the first four places at the finish), and the Cobras had merely to keep motoring steadily through the night to take the GT category, the challenge from privately-owned Ferraris having evaporated early on. Sharing one car with Bondurant, Schlesser began driving too enthusiastically for Alan Mann's taste. 'All the "slow" signals in the world had no effect so I brought him in to the pits, told him to get out of the car, and threatened to replace him by Allen Grant. He was okay after that—but his wife

CHAPTER FOUR

Side by side, Sears/Whitmore and Bondurant/Schlesser take the flag from 'Toto' Roche at Reims to clinch the GT championship for Cobra. Bondurant had come 5th overall, winning the GT category; Sears was 2nd in the class with only seven rods and pistons in his engine!

threw a bottle of champagne at me.' And Bondurant/Schlesser finished fifth overall to win the category and clinch the Division III GT championship. The Shelby/Ford publicity campaign made much of the race having finished on 4 July, Independence Day, and apparently saw no irony in the fact that, far from being independent, they had been almost completely dependent on their British team manager.

A sidelight on the Reims achievement was provided by Sears and Whitmore, who finished ninth overall and second in class—on seven cylinders! Their car threw a conrod when Sears was driving: 'It just went bang, so I declutched quickly and pushed it for what seemed a *very* long way to the pits.' There, Jabby Crombac of *Autosport* remarked to Alan Mann that it was a pity they had to retire. 'I asked if he'd bet me 100 bottles of champagne that we couldn't finish, and he agreed. So we pulled out the remains of that rod, took out the pushrods from that cylinder, and clamped two bearing caps on the journal. It ran quite well, really . . . and we won the champagne.'

There remained two European events, the Coppa di Enna in Sicily and a French hillclimb (of no championship significance to the Mann team because maximum hillclimb points had already been scored at Rossfeld), plus the final race at Bridgehampton, NY. The Coppa di Enna was a curious race on a road circuit running around the lake of Pergusa, which classical mythology tells us was magically formed by Pluto (no relation to the Walt Disney character of that name) to cover his retreat when he carried Persephone off to his underground lair. Legend has it that the waters of the lake are filled with serpents, but the Cobras stayed on dry land to take a class 1-2 ahead of a Ferrari. Finally, Bob Johnson won the GT category at Bridgehampton in mid-September with another Cobra; no Ferraris were entered.

Two months later, a specially built $75,000 publicity caravan began a 5000-mile tour of twelve major US cities with a Cobra coupé, a Ford GT40, a GT350 Shelby Mustang and a Cobra 427 Mark III. In page after page of publicity handouts, not a single mention was made of AC Cars Ltd or Alan Mann Racing when trumpeting 'the first American car to win a World Championship trophy'. Alan Mann remains unconcerned, taking a realistic attitude to the ballyhoo. 'My job was simply to win what I was told to try and win, and thus get publicity for Ford, not myself—and I was quite well paid to do it. Remember, I was outside the political net. The politics in Ford Division were much heavier than you could

CHAPTER FOUR

Shelby talk: the caravan that toured the USA proclaimed the Cobra as 1965 World Champion, the car 'that beat Europe's best', taking first place at Daytona, Sebring, Monza, the TT, Nürburgring, Rossfeld, Reims, Enna and Bridgehampton. This wasn't true, any of it—but it certainly sounded good. And everyone believed what they wanted to believe

imagine—people's jobs depended on certain things—but when they sent me cars, money, what I did and how I did it was my business; politically, all the guys in Detroit could wash their hands of it if I made some enormous cock-up. Ford stayed well behind the front line until afterwards, when we'd won the championship for them.'

And yet, although Alan Mann is such a pragmatist in regard to the championship, there is one thing that he still resents even today, 20 years later. 'At the end of the season the cars came back from Sicily in pretty rough shape, as you can imagine. I must have had them at my place for fully three months while I wrote letters to the States asking what I was to do with them, and I very nearly had to scrap the lot to avoid paying Customs duty on them. But nobody cared. Ford Division didn't want them, Shelby didn't want them—they were just last year's junk.'

Specifications

Note: There are considerable discrepancies in published Cobra specifications, and in the selection of catalogue and road test specifications quoted below, it will be seen that some figures are clearly incorrect.

Original specification sheet (9 April 1962):

Wheelbase: 90 in. (2286 mm)
Front track: 51 in. (1295 mm)
Rear track: 48 in. (1219 mm)
Overall length: 167 in. (4242 mm)
Width: 60 in. (1524 mm)
Height: 46 in. (1168 mm) to top of screen
Kerb weight: 2100 lbs (955 kg)
Engine type: Ford V8, ohv, 260 cid (4261 cc). Bore and stroke, 3.8 in. (96.52 mm) by 2.875 in. (73.03 mm). Power output: 260 bhp (194.5 Kw) at 5800 rpm (optional versions giving up to 335 bhp (250.6 Kw)). Torque: 269 lb ft (371.89 Nm) at 4800 rpm.
Features: All-aluminium hand-formed body; genuine leather upholstery; individual bucket seats; adjustable steering wheel; full instrumentation (tachometer, speedometer, oil pressure, oil temperature, water temperature, ammeter); 12 in. Girling disc brakes with dual master cylinders; choice of final-drive ratios from 2.72:1 to 4.56:1; full road equipment (safety glass windscreen, folding top and side curtains, turn indicators, etc). Heater/defroster and radio optional at extra cost.

Road & Track, September 1962

Wheelbase: 90 in. (2286 mm)
Front track: 51.5 in. (1308 mm)
Rear track: 52.5 in. (1334 mm)
Overall length: 151.5 in. (3848 mm)
Width: 61 in. (1549 mm)

SPECIFICATIONS

Height: 49 in. (1245 mm)
Kerb weight: 2020 lb (918 kg)
Engine type and features as above. Tyre size: 6.50/6.70–15. Gear ratios 1.0, 1.41, 1.78 and 2.36:1. Final drive, 3.54:1.

Autosport, 7 June 1963

As above but kerb weight = 2016 lb (916 kg). Engine type 289 cid (4736 cc). Bore and Stroke: 4.0 in. (101.6 mm) by 2.87 in. (72.9 mm). Power output, 275 bhp (206 Kw). Compression ratio, 9.2:1. Four-choke downdraught carburetter. Borg-Warner 4-speed, all-synchro gearbox. Hypoid final drive, ratio 3.77:1, with self-locking differential. Ladder-type tubular frame. Independent suspension front and rear by transverse leaf springs and wishbones with telescopic dampers and anti-roll torsion bars front and rear. Rack and pinion steering. Equipment includes speedometer, rev counter, oil and water thermometers, oil pressure and fuel gauges, ammeter, clock, flashing indicators, heating and demisting, windscreen wipers and washers.

Road & Track, June 1964

As Sept 1962 specification, but kerb weight = 2170 lb (986 kg). Engine type 289 cid: power output = 271 bhp (203 Kw) at 6000 rpm; torque = 314 lb ft (434 Nm) at 3400 rpm. Compression ratio, 11.6:1. Final drive, 3.77:1. Tyre size, 7.35 × 15. Instruments: 160 mph speedometer, 8000 rpm tachometer, oil temp, water temp, oil pressure, fuel, clock, ammeter. Included at list price: wire wheels and limited-slip differential. Available at extra cost: grille guard, wind wings, visors, heater, seat belts, luggage rack, chrome wheels, outside mirror, radio, plus performance options.

Autocar, 12 November 1965 (Mark II, UK spec)

Wheelbase: 90 in. (2286 mm)
Front track: 53.5 in. (1359 mm)
Rear track: 53.75 in. (1365 mm)
Overall length: 158 in. (4013 mm)
Width: 63 in. (1600 mm)
Height: 48 in. (1219 mm) to top of hood
Kerb weight: 2315 lb (1052 kg)
Engine type, 289 cid: power output = 300 bhp gross (224 Kw) at 5750 rpm; torque = 285 lb ft gross (394 Nm) at 4500 rpm.
Final drive = 3.54:1 (Salisbury Powr-Lok differential). Tyre size, 185–15. Girling disc brakes, diameter 11.7 in. (297 mm) front, 10.75 in. (273 mm) rear. Heater and screenwasher standard equipment.

SPECIFICATIONS

Shelby specification sheet, 1 April 1965 (Mark III 427)

Wheelbase: 90 in. (2286 mm)
Front track: 56 in. (1422 mm)
Rear track: 56 in. (1422 mm)
Overall length: 156 in. (3962 mm)
Width: 68 in. (1727 mm)
Height: 49 in. (1245 mm)
Kerb weight: 2150 lb (977 kg)
Engine type, 427 cid (6997 cc). Bore and Stroke, 4.24 in. (107.7 mm) by 3.788 in. (96.22 mm). Power output, 390 bhp (292 Kw) at 5200 rpm. Torque, 475 lb ft (657 Nm) at 3700 rpm. Compression ratio, 10.0:1. Tyre size, 8.15 × 15. Final drive, 3.54:1.

Shelby specification sheet, 18 April 1966

As above, but kerb weight = 2529 lb (1150 kg).
Independent suspension front and rear using large coil springs. Hydraulic shock absorber units, 'incorporated in highly-developed design which virtually eliminates dive and squat'. Final drive ratio, 3.31:1

Motor, 14 October 1967 ('AC 289' European model)

Wheelbase: 90 in. (2386 mm)
Front track: 54.25 in. (1378 mm)
Rear track: 54 in. (1372 mm)
Overall length: 159 in. (4039 mm)
Width: 65 in. (1651 mm)
Height: 48 in. (1219 mm)
Kerb weight: 2353 lb (1069 kg).
Engine type, 289 cid: power output, 271 bhp gross (203 Kw) at 6000 rpm; torque, 312 lb ft (431 Nm) at 3400 rpm. Compression ratio, 11.0:1. Gear ratios, 1.0, 1.31, 1.66 and 2.20:1. Final drive, 3.54:1.
Independent suspension by coil springs and wishbones, with Armstrong telescopic shock absorbers.

Road & Track, July 1974 (Mark III 427)

As Shelby specifications, but kerb weight = 2530 lb (1150 kg).
Power output, 425 bhp gross (318 Kw) at 6000 rpm. Torque, 480 lb ft gross (664 Nm) at 3700 rpm.

Acknowledgements

Of the many, many people who have kindly helped me with this book I must single out three for special mention: they are Karl Ludvigsen, who loaned me his reference files on the Cobra, and Barrie and June Bird, who invited me to spend a weekend at their home while I was studying the Bird collection of AC material, while Barrie also read the entire book in manuscript and made many valuable comments and suggestions. I am also indebted to Brian Angliss, Klaus Arning, John Atkins, Roger Bell, Eileen Brockbank, Gordon Bruce, David Burgess-Wise, John Cooper, Lord Cross, Cliff Davis, Vin Davison, Tony Dron, Philip Garnett Keeler, Brian Gilbert-Smith, David Hescroff, Derek Hurlock, Keith Judd, Rod Leach, Russell Lowry, Wally Marshall, Stuart Mathieson, Cameron Millar, David Peers, Cyril Posthumus, Phil Remington, Ian Richardson, Jim Rose, Ken Rudd, Jack Sears, Tom Threlfall, John Tojeiro, Alan Turner, David Watson and Paul Woudenberg.

The journals consulted were *Autocar*, *Autocourse*, *Autosport*, *Auto Sports*, *Motor*, *Motor Sport* and *Newsweek*. Books included *AC* by Martyn Watkins (Foulis), *AC Cobra* by Anthony Pritchard and Keith Davey (Profile Publications), *Carroll Shelby's Racing Cobra* by Dave Friedman and John Christy (Osprey Publishing), *Castrol Racing Driver's Manual* by Frank Gardner and Doug Nye (Patrick Stephens Ltd), *Ford Cobra Guide* by Bill Carroll (TAB Books), *Motoring* by A. E. Berriman (Methuen), *Specials* by John Bolster (Foulis), *Such Sweet Thunder* by John Blunsden and David Phipps (Motor Racing Publications), *Track Tests* by Michael Bowler (Hamlyn) and *World Sports Car Championship* by Cyril

ACKNOWLEDGEMENTS

Posthumus (MacGibbon and Kee). Organizations that proved particularly helpful were the National Motor Museum Library at Beaulieu, the Chichester Library (Reference Section), Ford Motor Co Ltd in Britain and the Shelby American Automobile Club in the USA.

My wife Caroline translated from American into English for me when necessary, and also took many of the pictures, including the cover shot of David Corben's superbly rebuilt Mark II. For the remaining pictures I am indebted to AC Cars PLC, Autosport, Barrie Bird, Cliff Davis, Vin Davison, Ford Motor Company, Guy Griffiths, Karl Ludvigsen, Tim Parker, Maurice Rowe of *Motor*, Ken Rudd, Fred Scatley, John Tojeiro and Alan Turner.

Index

A
AC Cars Ltd 8, 18, 20, 23, 25, 34, 35, 36, 39, 58, 59, 61, 73, 77, 121, 127
  2 litre six 20, 23
  2 litre saloon 27
  Ace 8, 22, 23, 26, 27, 32, 34–37, 41, 43, 45, 79, 82
  Ace-Bristol 29, 31, 34, 42, 50
  Aceca 25, 29, 32, 35, 36, 41, 59
  Auto-Carrier 18
  Bristol 59, 81
  Buckland 14, 17
  Greyhound 32–34, 36, 41, 59
  Sociable 17–19
Abarth 109
Agapion, Charlie 114
Alfa Romeo 105
All American Racers Inc. 57
Allard, Sydney 10, 41
Amon, Chris 94
Angliss, Brian 104
Arning, Klaus 57, 58
Aston Martin 16, 105
Autocar 34, 77, 78, 100, 102
Autocourse 105
Autokraft 55, 104
Autosport 17, 29, 31, 100, 121, 127

B
BMW 29
Bailey, Ernie 13, 17, 19
Belgian 24 Hours 105
Bell, Roger 103
Bentley 89
Berger, Georges 29, 31
Berriman, A. E. 79
Bird, Barrie 8, 43, 90
Bolster, John 9, 31, 100–102
Bolton, Peter 29, 31, 88, 92, 112
Bondurant, Bob 115, 116, 119–121, 124–126
Bowler, Michael 82, 103
Brands Hatch 94

Bridgehampton NY race 127
Bristol Aeroplane Company 29, 36
British Saloon Car Championship 88
Brock, Peter 106, 109, 110
Brockbank, Eileen 91
Bruce, Hon. Victor 19
Buick 36, 50

C
Cadillac 41, 84
California Metal Shaping 108
Carerra Panamericana 105
Castle Combe 15, 16
Challenge Mondial 108
Chapman, Colin 93
Chrysler 35
Cooper 10, 29
  Charles 12, 22
  John 12, 22
Cooper-MG 14–16
Coppa di Enna 127, 128
Coupe Sport 108
Crombac, Jabby 127
Cross, Lord 77

D
Daimler V8 36
Davis, Cliff 14–16, 20, 22, 29, 83, 89, 90
Davison, Vin 14, 17, 20, 21, 23, 25
Daytona coupé 85, 88, 89, 106, 109, 110, 112, 124
Daytona 93, 102, 111, 128
Dutch GP 16
Dymock, Eric 98

E
Edge, S. F. 19
Elva 10
England, Lofty 36

F
FIA 105
FIA Chqmpionnat du Monde des Constructeurs 105
Ferrari, Enzo 7, 8, 29, 111, 115
Ferrari 105, 111, 125, 127
  166 Barchetta 15
  250LM 111
  275GTB 111, 124
  250GTO 88, 90, 111, 114, 119, 120, 123
Feutel, Ed 103
Fiat 12, 15, 22
Ford Motor Company 43, 64, 78, 105 et passim to 123
  Cortina GT 112
  Fairlane 103
  Falcon 112
  GT40 120, 127
  Mustang 41, 50, 58, 78, 86, 112
  Zephyr 34, 73
Frazer Nash 16
Frua 50, 97

G
GT Championship 109, 111
Gardner, Frank 85, 118
General Motors 38
Gomm, Maurice 31
Goodwood 16, 29
Grant, Allen 117, 118, 120, 121, 125
Grant Jerry 121
Greene, Sid 16
Guards Trophy 94
Guinness Book of Records 103
Gurney, Dan 45

H
HWM 10
Healey, Donald 41
Henderson, Jock 38
Hill, Phil 45

134

INDEX

Hogg, Tony 83, 100, 102
Holman, John 112
Hugus, Ed 64
Hurlock, Charles 19, 34
   Derek 8, 34, 37, 38, 57, 59, 112
   William 19

J
JAP 12
Jaguar 38, 105
   D type 29
   E type 42, 88
   Mark 10 42
Jenkinson, Denis 83
Johnson, Bob 121, 125, 127
Jowett Jupiter 12
Judd, Keith 73, 77

K
Kieft 10

L
Lagonda 3 litre 22
Lancia 105
Le Mans 29, 31, 33, 88, 91, 92, 101, 110, 114, 119, 121, 125
Lea-Francis 13, 17, 20, 21
Leonard, Lionel 13, 15
Lindbergh, Charles 7
Lister, Brian 10, 12
Ljungfeldt, Bo 120, 121
London Motor Show 20–22, 29, 32
Lotus 10, 29, 105

M
MG 12, 13, 14
MIRA 98, 103
Mann, Alan 85, 112, 117, 119–121, 124, 125, 127, 128
Marczewski 20, 35
Marlboro 12 Hours 112
Maserati 16, 29, 105
Mathieson, Stuart 115
McNally, Patrick 121
Mercury 41
Miles, Ken 50
Mille Miglia 105
Monte Carlo Rally 19, 112
Monza 1000 Kilometres 112, 120, 127

Moon, Dean 73
Morton, John 50
Moss, Stirling 91
Motor 27, 34, 78, 82, 84, 98, 99, 100, 102
Motor Sport 83

N
Neerpasch, Jochen 115, 122, 124
Negstadt, Bob 57
New York Motor Show 39
Nürburgring 105, 112, 120, 124, 128

O
Orange County Raceway 104
Osca 105
Oulton Park 118

P
Parkes, Mike 88
Patthey, Hubert 29, 31
Payne, Tom 121, 125
Pon, Ben 120
Porsche 105, 109, 111, 119
   904 114, 120, 121
Portwine, John 18

R
RAC Rally 19, 20
Reims 12 Hours 125, 126, 128
Reventlow, Lance 73
Richardson, Ian 90
Riverside Raceway 96, 109
Road & Track 83, 93, 100, 102–104, 121
Remington, Phil 8, 57, 96
Roche, Toto 126
Rossfeld hillclimb 120, 127, 128
Rover 36
Rudd, Ken 27, 29, 34, 35, 77, 81, 100
RuddSpeed 35

S
Salvadori, Roy 81
Sanderson, David 37, 88, 92
Scarab 73
Schlesser, Jo 115, 121, 125, 126
Scott-Brown, Archie 13

Sears, Chris 13
Sears, Jack 88, 94, 112, 115, 117, 119–121, 124, 126
   Stanley 88
Sebring 54, 111, 113, 128
   12 Hours 104
Shelby American Automobile Club 76
Shelby American Cobra 6, 55, 59
Shelby, Carroll 8, 35–39, 41–43, 45, 57, 59, 62, 73, 103, 105, 112, 126
Shelby Mustang 57, 127
Sidney, Harold 20
Silverstone 88, 96
Smith, Dick 103
Stratton, Desmond 20
Stoop, Dickie 31
Sunbeam TT 89
Sunday Times 91
Sutcliffe, Peter 119, 120, 123

T
TVR Tuscan 102
Targa Florio 120
Thompson, Dick 121, 123, 124
Thoroughbred and Classic Cars 103
Threlfall, Chris 12
Tojeiro, John 10–14, 17, 20, 22, 23, 31, 32
   Bristol 14, 16, 89, 90
   Special 21, 25, 33
Tour de France 112
Tourist Trophy 31, 88, 105, 119, 128
Turner, Alan 20, 23, 29, 33, 34, 46, 57, 58, 73, 93, 96, 110, 112

U
Uren, Jeff 88

W
Weller, John 18, 19
Whiteaway 29
Whitmore, John 115, 117–120, 123, 126
Willment Racing 88, 94, 118
Wolseley 12
Woolfe, John 99, 101, 103
World Sports Car Championship 105

135

COBRA
WORLD CHAMPION
SCHEDULE
LOS ANGELES NOV. 17
SAN FRANCISCO NOV. 18
KANSAS CITY NOV. 23
DALLAS NOV. 26
CHICAGO NOV. 30
DETROIT DEC. 2
CLEVELAND DEC. 4
ATLANTA DEC. 8
CHARLOTTE DEC. 10
WASHINGTON DEC. 13
NEW YORK DEC. 15
PROVIDENCE DEC. 17
FOR THE STORY BEHIND
THE AMERICAN CHAMPION
THAT BEAT EUROPE'S BEST....
READ
THE COBRA STORY
by Carroll Shelby
AT YOUR BOOK STORE NOW!
VH 4336